Formerly
New Directions for
Mental Health Services

Editor-in-chief

NEW DIRECTIONS FOR YOUTH DEVELOPMENT

Theory
Practice
Research

winter | 2003

Understanding the Social Worlds of Immigrant Youth

D1566116

Carola Suárez-Orozco
Irina L. G. Todorova

issue
editors

JOSSEY-BASS
A Wiley Imprint
www.josseybass.com

UNDERSTANDING THE SOCIAL WORLDS OF IMMIGRANT YOUTH
Carola Suárez-Orozco, Irina L. G. Todorova (eds.)
New Directions for Youth Development, No. 100, Winter 2003
Gil G. Noam, Editor-in-Chief

Microfilm copies of issues and articles are available in 16mm and 35mm, as well as microfiche in 105mm, through University Microfilms Inc., 300 North Zeeb Road, Ann Arbor, Michigan 48106-1346.

NEW DIRECTIONS FOR YOUTH DEVELOPMENT (ISSN 1533-8916, electronic ISSN 1537-5781) is part of The Jossey-Bass Psychology Series and is published quarterly by Wiley Subscription Services, Inc., A Wiley company, at Jossey-Bass, 989 Market Street, San Francisco, California 94103-1741. POSTMASTER: Send address changes to New Directions for Youth Development, Jossey-Bass, 989 Market Street, San Francisco, California 94103-1741.

SUBSCRIPTIONS cost $80.00 for individuals and $160.00 for institutions, agencies, and libraries. Prices subject to change. Refer to the order form at the back of this issue.

EDITORIAL CORRESPONDENCE should be sent to the Editor-in-Chief, Dr. Gil G. Noam, Harvard Graduate School of Education, Larsen Hall 601, Appian Way, Cambridge, MA 02138 or McLean Hospital, 115 Mill Street, Belmont, MA 02478.

Cover photograph by Digital Vision.

www.josseybass.com

Contents

     Through a detailed case study, this chapter illustrates the multiple social influences that support and challenge immigrant youth in the United States and introduces the themes of many of the following contributions.

     Children in a Mexican immigrant community provide essential help to their families, including translating, interpreting, and providing sibling care. These daily life activities shape possibilities for learning and development.

     The authors examine the role of two distinct school contexts within the same school that shape the academic outcomes of Vietnamese students as they contend with the pressures of being considered members of the "model minority."

     This chapter examines ethnic language schools and the system of supplementary education in the immigrant Chinese community in the United States by considering how ethnic community organizations contribute to educational achievement.

Editor-in-Chief's Notes

MIGRATION AND IMMIGRATION are worldwide phenomena of huge proportion. Considering the resulting changes for millions of people, it is quite surprising how little we know about the experience of growing up as an immigrant youth and about the process of creating a new life in a new country. Is the adjustment pattern different for various cultural and ethnic groups? How much do age and gender matter? On the psychological level, what is the balance between enduring loss and risk and creating resilience and a rich inner life?

Too often the immigration experience is viewed from a pathology perspective—the loss of home, culture, and identity. *Yearning*, *marginalization*, and *prejudice* are terms we often use in relationship to immigrant families. At the same time we tend to idealize the opportunities of young people who move to the industrialized Western world, the landed immigrants in a world of opportunity. Both realities coexist in the immigration experience described in this issue of New Directions for Youth Development, which focuses primarily on immigrant children and adolescents growing up in the United States.

I chose this topic for this issue for both personal and professional reasons. By the time I turned fifteen I had lived in three cultures and countries with four different languages, each time as an immigrant. The immigration experience was a chronic one, marked not only by difficult beginnings but also by fascinating encounters and discoveries. I was a young adult when I settled in the United States, beginning a modern and quite prevalent form of immigration—living in the new country while maintaining a bridge to the old. These sets of experiences convinced me that globalized forms of

NEW DIRECTIONS FOR YOUTH DEVELOPMENT, NO. 100, WINTER 2003 © WILEY PERIODICALS, INC.

youth culture are increasingly associated with the cross-cultural migratory patterns of present life.

Professionally, I became interested in how youth construct their identities and began a small action research project with my colleague and friend Anthony Appiah. Anthony and I conducted long-term group discussion sessions with children in a Boston neighborhood that had a large proportion of immigrants among its population. While not all of the students in the groups were immigrants, many had come to the United States as young children or had been born in the United States shortly after their parents arrived from the Caribbean, Southeast Asia, or Mexico. We were interested in how the globalized youth culture of music, dress, and media would interact with the experiences of cultural identity, heritage, and migration. We were privileged to be allowed into the experiential world of these young adolescents who gave so freely of themselves and inducted us into their worlds of fear and retaliation, aspiration and motivation.

We discovered a three-level reality: At the outer crust, the differences in background and migration mattered, and kids took note of their differences and their backgrounds. They made surprisingly little reference to them, however. They were not particularly interested in who came from where, who was born where, and even who had what kind of skin color. They were far more interested in commonality, the second level of experience we detected, where the common features of youth culture, of media tastes and music choice, of clothing, and so on mattered far more than any distinctions between them. Youth culture, in the mind of these kids, was the great democratizer, the space that united them beyond their differences.

A third, more hidden level of experience emerged as we got deeper and listened to the various themes that emerged. What we heard at that level were many concerns about family life, neighborhoods, and communities that showed us how much these youngsters were making sense of the various and often contradictory cultures they inhabited. We were struck by how complex the act of bridging really was for them, though they always seemed set on portraying their struggles as normative and "not a big deal." Theirs were often stories of loyalty to home, culture, and background in a world portrayed as cool, uncaring, and dangerous.

Our qualitative work was part of a movement of researching immigrant youth. Despite a rapidly expanding body of research, there is still far too little interdisciplinary work done that deals with children and adolescents who migrate to new countries. It is also hard to find good research that simultaneously is practical and helps the practitioner keep up with newest thinking. The issue editors, Carola Suárez-Orozco and Irina L. G. Todorova, were able to assemble an impressive group of scholars, many of whom represent the leadership of the growing field of immigration research. They combine clinical and developmental psychology perspectives, as well as anthropology, education, and to some degree sociology. The topics are far-reaching and extremely relevant—school, media, religion, and so on—and the methods used are both quantitative and qualitative. Above all, the chapters are readable and original and provide much food for thought for policymakers, funders, practitioners, and scholars who make up the diverse readership we attempt to connect through the journal.

I want to end by thanking Phyllis Wentworth for her major work as editorial manager of this issue as well as of the previous issue, "Deconstructing the School-to-Prison Pipeline" (New Directions for Youth Development, no. 99). Phyllis was involved at all levels of the editorial process and both issues are stronger because of her insights and attention to detail.

Gil G. Noam
Editor-in-Chief

Issue Editors' Notes

IMMIGRANT YOUTH are increasingly found in neighborhoods, schools, community centers, and health care facilities all over the country. These youth are largely of Latino, Asian, or Caribbean origins and represent a wide range of cultural, linguistic, and racial backgrounds. Despite the magnitude of the phenomenon, only in the last two decades has systematic comparative research begun to focus on their experiences.

Anthropologist Clyde Kluckhohn noted that a man is at once like all other men, like some other men, and like no other man. The same holds true for immigrant youth. In some ways they are like all other children—immigrant and nonimmigrant alike. They also share particular traits and experiences that are unique to the immigrant experience—an immigrant youth from India often has more in common with an immigrant youth from Colombia than she does with an adolescent who never left Calcutta or one who is of mainstream American origin and has always resided in Indianapolis. At the same time, of course, all immigrant youth have distinctive features common only to their own unique experience. An interesting intellectual exercise with clear social implications given the magnitude of the phenomenon is to search for common denominators that characterize the immigrant youth experience. Shedding light on these issues has relevance to those who provide service to immigrant youth in educational, community, and clinical settings, as well as for policymakers who will enact legislation that will in important ways determine the circumstances and opportunities available to immigrant youth.

Research focusing on immigrant youth in recent years has mostly examined educational outcomes—certainly an important predictor of adjustment to a new society. Much of this research pays

NEW DIRECTIONS FOR YOUTH DEVELOPMENT, NO. 100, WINTER 2003 © WILEY PERIODICALS, INC.

particularly close attention to such domains as second language acquisition and bilingualism. Within the clinical literature in psychology and family therapy, of particular interest is the tension that arises between the parental culture of origin and that of the new social context—how do immigrant youth come to terms with these divergences, contradictions, and competing cultural models?

There is little work that systematically considers the multiple social worlds in which immigrant youth develop.[1] What are the social contexts in which immigrant youth find themselves? How salient are these contexts to the youth? How might these contexts influence changing identities and educational and well-being outcomes? As we will show in the introductory chapter, a critical feature of immigration is the disruption of the networks of relations available to the youth: loved ones are almost always left behind, children are often separated for long periods from parents and siblings before rejoining them in the new country, and new contexts may present few or not necessarily healthy social choices. Of particular relevance are the following issues: Who and what are the guides to the rules of engagement in the new society? What are the models of appropriate and sanctioned behaviors in the new land? What are the sources of social support providing information, tangible help, and emotional encouragement? Who do immigrant youth turn to as they forge new identities that may allow them to integrate successfully into the new society? This issue of *New Directions for Youth Development* is devoted to exploring these issues.

The Social Worlds of Immigrant Youth offers an opportunity to explore in detail some of the major social influences that help shape immigrant children's paths in their journey in the United States. In this volume we provide a glimpse into the complex social realities that immigrant youth encounter. These chapters provide a comparative perspective by examining a wide range of immigrant groups. The first chapter, by issue editors Carola Suárez-Orozco and Irina Todorova, frames the ways in which networks of relations are disrupted by migration and examines the significant role that networks of social relations play in the lives of immigrant youth.

Marjorie Faulstich Orellana, in Chapter Two, considers the home lives of Mexican immigrant youth, with a particular focus on the essential contributions these youth make within their families. In reading this chapter it is interesting to consider how these activities structure the children's time, as well as how their roles may influence their emerging sense of self. In Chapter Three, Gilberto Conchas and Cristina Pérez provide insight into the role that two distinct social contexts play in shaping the academic outcomes of Vietnamese students. Min Zhou and Xi-Yuan Li, in Chapter Four, present new data on Chinese language schools. Placing the emergence of these centers within a historical framework, the authors demonstrate the ways in which these after-school educational enclaves foster academic achievement among their participants.

The next three chapters present new materials emerging from the five-year interdisciplinary Longitudinal Immigrant Student Adaptation (LISA) study funded by the National Science Foundation, the W.T. Grant Foundation, and the Spencer Foundation and directed by Carola Suárez-Orozco and Marcelo Suárez-Orozco of the Harvard Graduate School of Education. This study followed the lives of four hundred newly arrived immigrant youth from five regions, including China, Central America, the Dominican Republic, Haiti, and Mexico. The LISA study utilized a variety of methods, including structured student and parent interviews, ethnographic observations, projective and objective measures, reviews of school records and behavior checklists, as well as teacher questionnaires and interviews. The chapters based on this study that are presented in this volume were developed by advanced doctoral students who worked as research assistants and data analysts for the project. In Chapter Five, Nora E. Thompson and Andrea G. Gurney examine a neglected area of research—the significant role of religion in the lives of most immigrant youth. Desirée Baolian Qin-Hilliard, in Chapter Six, demonstrates how academic performance is a highly gendered process of psychosocial adaptation. She considers the role that socially prescribed gendered expectations, restrictions, and contexts play in the schooling of immigrant boys and girls. Finally, in Chapter Seven, Josephine Louie examines the social world of media—increasingly recognized as a significant socializing agent in the lives of youth. Louie presents data on the patterns of media consumption of immigrant youth coming from a variety of countries, considering a wide range of media-use patterns, including exposures to ethnic and mainstream media and the varieties of social environments in which immigrant youth view television.

As our population of immigrant youth continues to grow, the ways in which they are incorporated into our society become ever more important for the future of our economy, society, and culture. The changing social worlds of immigrant youth are highly influential in their development. Hence, it is puzzling that scholars of human development have neglected this important domain of inquiry. The intent of this volume is to present new and heretofore unpublished data that will deepen understanding of the social worlds of immigrant youth among researchers, practitioners, and policymakers interested in facilitating positive development of this growing sector of our youth population.

Carola Suárez-Orozco
Irina L. G. Todorova
Issue Editors

Note

1. For important contributions on the social influences on immigrant youth, see Phelan, P., Davidson, A. L., and Yu, H. C. (1993). Students' multiple worlds: Navigating the borders of family, peer, and social cultures. In P. Phelan & A. L. Davidson (Eds.), *Renegotiating cultural diversity in American schools* (pp. 52–88). New York: Teachers College Press; and Stanton-Salazar, R. D. (2001). Manufacturing hope and despair: The school and kin support networks of U.S.-Mexican youth. New York: Teachers College Press.

CAROLA SUÁREZ-OROZCO *is codirector of the Harvard Immigration Project at the Harvard Graduate School of Education and Scholar in Residence at the Ross Institute in East Hampton, New York.*

IRINA L. G. TODOROVA *is a postdoctoral fellow with the Harvard Immigration Project at the Harvard Graduate School of Education.*

Executive Summary

Chapter One: The social worlds of immigrant youth

Carola Suárez-Orozco, Irina L. G. Todorova

Because first- and second-generation immigrant youth currently constitute 20 percent of the children growing up in the United States, their healthy development has fundamental long-term implications for our society. Immigrant youth undergo a host of changes that can have lasting impacts on their development. Their journeys follow complex paths—often bifurcating into divergent experiences and varied outcomes. Some youth thrive through immigration; others struggle to cope. In this introductory chapter, a detailed case study is used to illustrate the interconnection of multiple social influences in one particular youth's path of migration. The chapter further identifies some of the major influences on immigrant youth development, including the stresses of migration, family separations and reunifications, changing networks of relations, poverty and segregation, and the challenges of identity formation.

Chapter Two: Responsibilities of children in Latino immigrant homes

Marjorie Faulstich Orellana

Children's contributions to household functioning (including general household help as well as specific work as translators and

NEW DIRECTIONS FOR YOUTH DEVELOPMENT, NO. 100, WINTER 2003 © WILEY PERIODICALS, INC.

interpreters) in a Mexican immigrant community near Chicago are examined. Survey and observational data situate the enriched descriptions within a portrait of broader social trends. These data document gendered divisions of labor in homes as well as the relationship between engagement in translating work and school achievement. New directions for policy and practice that build on cultural belief systems and better leverage the skills that immigrant children acquire through their household contributions are suggested.

Chapter Three: Surfing the "model minority" wave of success: How the school context shapes distinct experiences among Vietnamese youth

Gilberto Q. Conchas, Cristina C. Pérez

The authors present a qualitative case study that explores how and why twenty-seven immigrant and native-born Vietnamese high school students attained academic success despite social and economic barriers. These youth benefited from the "model minority" label ascribed to "Asian" students in two significant ways: first, as a result of adult expectations, these Vietnamese students gained structural and ideological advantages over other nonwhite racial groups; and second, individually and collectively, consciously and subconsciously, they reinforced the "model minority" image as they attempted to attain educational mobility. The students differed, however, in how they responded to the model minority construct depending on the school contexts in which they were involved. Distinct types of academic programs forged complex and interrelated forms of student agency that differed along race and gender lines. The positive impact of community solidarity and networking along with exposure to students of different ethnicities and cultures suggest models of success for urban youth.

Chapter Four: Ethnic language schools and the development of supplementary education in the immigrant Chinese community in the United States

Min Zhou, Xi-Yuan Li

This chapter seeks to unpack ethnicity through a close examination of ethnic language schools and the ethnic system of supplementary education in the immigrant Chinese community in the United States. It is argued that ethnicity cannot be simplified into either a structural or a cultural measure. Rather, it encompasses values and behavioral patterns that are constantly interacting with both internal and external structural circumstances. It sheds light on the specific ways in which ethnic community organizations contribute to educational achievement.

Chapter Five: "He is everything": Religion's role in the lives of immigrant youth

Nora E. Thompson, Andrea G. Gurney

In this study, immigrant youth express in their own words the many ways in which religion plays a part in their lives. The process of immigration exposes youth to many specific stressors and challenges their sense of self-efficacy. Drawing on data collected by the Harvard Longitudinal Immigrant Adaptation study, immigrant youth reveal how they experience religion as protective in times of stress. Participants describe a sense of power and help attainable through prayer or ritual, and how, during a time when familiar contexts, relationships, and roles have been lost, religion provides them with a sense of continuity. The youth also share how they perceive religion providing them with protections from the risks of urban poverty, including the allure of drugs, early sexual activity, and violence, by offering them a clear boundary between right and wrong.

Chapter Six: Gendered expectations and gendered experiences: Immigrant students' adaptation in schools

Desirée Baolian Qin-Hilliard

An emerging theme in research on immigration and education is girls' tendency to outperform boys in schools. Few studies, however, have systematically examined why this gender pattern exists. In this chapter, the author examines the role of gender in immigrant students' adaptation in schools, drawing on data from the Longitudinal Immigrant Student Adaptation Study. Both quantitative and qualitative methods were used in the study. Her analyses show that over time girls receive higher grades and express higher future expectations than boys. She argues that immigrant girls are protected in their pursuit of education from risk factors, such as harsh school environments, by a supportive network of teachers, friends, and parents. These protective networks are less expansive and available to immigrant boys. Her analyses also demonstrate that over time boys are less likely than girls to maintain an identity tied to their country of origin. She speculates that immigrant girls may benefit from the shield of ethnicity more than their male counterparts.

Chapter Seven: Media in the lives of immigrant youth

Josephine Louie

Media researchers have long recognized that the mass media may play an important role in the socialization of youth. Recent national surveys suggest that U.S. teens spend significant amounts of time each day using a variety of communications media, such as television, radio, and the computer. Immigrant youth may have unique information needs and may be especially susceptible to the influences of the mass media as they adapt to life in their new country. This chapter examines media use trends among Chinese, Haitian, Dominican, Central American, and Mexican immigrant teens drawn from the Longitudinal Immigrant Student Adaptation Study at Harvard University. The data suggest that immigrant teens display media ownership levels similar to those of the U.S. teen population as a whole. At the same time, they appear more likely than the average U.S. teen to use media in the company of others and to consume a variety of ethnic-language media. Media exposure levels and content preferences also vary across immigrant groups and across genders. Those working with immigrant youth may help mediate the effects of media by discussing with youth and parents the media they consume and the messages they encounter.

This introductory chapter uses a detailed case study to illustrate the interconnection of multiple social influences on one particular youth's path of migration. It further identifies some of the major influences on immigrant youth development, including the stresses of migration, separations and reunifications, changing networks of relations, poverty and segregation, and identity formation.

1

The social worlds of immigrant youth

Carola Suárez-Orozco, Irina L. G. Todorova

DARIO is an adolescent of short stature with curly dark hair.[1] Always well groomed, he has big dark eyes, a chipped tooth, and a scar that dominates his face. He speaks in a raspy, monotone voice, rarely making eye contact. His manner is one of defiance and street savvy well beyond his years.

Dario arrived in the western United States from Central America at the age of ten. In a sad tale, relentlessly repeated, through the next few years he was fated to relive the trauma of the initial separation over and over again. He was first separated from his father when his parents divorced, followed by separation from his mother when she immigrated. Eight years later he left behind his beloved caretaking aunt to join his mother in the United States. This series of departures created ongoing confusion about loved ones and why they always disappear.

NEW DIRECTIONS FOR YOUTH DEVELOPMENT, NO. 100, WINTER 2003 © WILEY PERIODICALS, INC.

Both Dario and his mother speak about the hardships surrounding their separation and reunification. Attempts to reunite were unsuccessful for many years because of documentation issues. Dario recalls that when his visa was denied his mother was so upset she had to be taken to the hospital. It took eight years of efforts before he was able to join her, and during that time he saw his mother only twice. Undeniably, the separations were painful, but so were the reunifications. Dario's mother recalls that in the beginning there were times when Dario would call her at work, crying from fear and loneliness, requiring that she leave work early to be with him.

There is little stability in Dario's current living situation. When Dario arrived in the United States, his mother was in a relationship with a man he did not know. Dario formed a bond with his stepfather that lasted only a short while because his stepfather moved in and out of the home, before leaving permanently—another loss for Dario. In the meantime, two new siblings were born and a grandmother came to live with them, as well as a daughter of Dario's biological father. Despite the family's poverty, Dario's mother is raising four children.

The dynamic and unpredictable household membership, however, is somewhat mitigated by the family's network of social relations. As in many Latino homes, extended family, friends, and church-based relationships help the family in emotional and tangible ways. Dario and his mother define success in relational terms—as providing for immediate and extended family, as "giving back" for their efforts and sacrifices. The gauge of success is whether one has been able to be true to these principles of morality, responsibility to others, goodness, honesty, and authenticity.

Dario's vulnerability is further undermined by his neighborhood, where he is exposed to weapons, drugs, fights, and palpable tensions between ethnic groups. His attitude toward "the street" is ambivalence—he is both critical of and fascinated by it. While he acknowledges that the neighborhood is perceived as unsafe, he claims that he feels secure there. His mother worries that Dario "loves the street" and checks him for drug and alcohol possession when he comes home. She is concerned that she doesn't know his friends and their parents. Though there is no reason to think that Dario is involved with drugs or gangs, he is certainly at risk. It is "the street" that provides a space for him to construct an identity of competence, leadership, masculinity, and empowerment through his skill in sports—contrasting markedly with his experience in school.

Dario presents contrasting identities—one in the context of the classroom, where he is shy, obedient, and minimally engaged, and another in the street, where he livens up and appears in control. There is a striking disparity between his psychological vulnerability, sadness, and extreme shyness in the school context and the bravado he projects on the street.

This schism can be traced to his educational trajectory. Upon arrival in the United States, Dario was directed to a bilingual program. He was mainstreamed to a regular classroom two years later—a premature transition that reactivated unresolved previous losses. Leaving the "holding place" of the bilingual program is a difficult, disorienting, and anxiety-provoking transition for many immigrant children. For Dario this transition was complicated by the combination of his sadness from multiple losses that he carries with him and his still-limited English skills. His grades have plummeted and his engagement in school has suffered. The school pays no notice and the downward spiral continues. Dario's definition of academic achievement is behavioral and he holds true to that definition—his attendance is good, he is strict about handing in his homework, his teachers praise his behavior in the classroom. Nevertheless, they note that he often does not understand the material. Dario demonstrates how behavioral engagement in school is not enough. His efforts end in frustration; because of his limited language and unavailable academic supports, they do not lead to outcomes that are gratifying and do not encourage further academic efforts. Nevertheless, Dario is positive about school because he feels emotionally supported by relations with adults and peers. This has been particularly true in high school, where he has created a strong connection with one counselor—a relationship that is probably critical in keeping him in school. Unfortunately, his positive attitude has diminished over time, though it has never turned adversarial.

In terms of his ethnic identity, to borrow from poet Walt Whitman, Dario "contains multitudes."[2] When we first meet him, he considered himself to be an "American," although at the time he had lived in the United States for only one year, did not hold U.S. citizenship, and spoke almost no English. This identification is ambivalent because he confides that he believes that most Americans think Latinos are bad and troublemakers, and that in turn Latinos think Americans are racist. In his narrative we sense the tension between peers from different ethnic groups, and he reflects on the way Latino youth feel diminished in the eyes of the mainstream culture.

In time we have seen a shift into a multiple identity. Dario seems to be increasingly adapting to a style that incorporates customs from his original culture, from African American culture, and from mainstream American youth culture. His friends are mostly second-generation Latinos who understand but do not speak Spanish and maintain a value system deeply embedded in relationships. He identifies with the victimization and discrimination experienced by African Americans as well as with their strength and efforts for civil rights and justice. An important catalyst in this shift is the media—he watches MTV more than any other channel and considers talk show hosts as role models.

The immigration process has deeply affected Dario. Like his face, his social and psychological being are scarred—from multiple losses and separations, an unpredictable family situation, academic struggles, and discriminatory experiences. His process of adaptation is a process of identity shifts—from wounded to empowered and back, from the frustration of the classroom to perceived competence in the street.

Despite all the hardships, Dario demonstrates resilience and continues to strive. His resilience is fueled from two main sources. One is relational—he has supportive friends, counselors, and connections with extended family. In his relationships he is friendly, respectful, and responsible. The other aspect of his resilience is that of persistence and hope. He is still in school, he continues to try, he has aspirations, he is not hostile toward school and family. He is fascinated by street life but is not in gangs. He has not rejected academic goals.

Dario's story highlights the complex ways in which social and psychological influences interweave to shape immigrant children's paths in the United States. Dario is a child "hanging by a thread." In many ways he appears to have adjusted remarkably well, but the balance is fragile. For many immigrant youth, social influences have conspired in ways that have caused the threads to sever. For others, the threads have aligned to reinforce and weave together a process of social and academic adaptation.

Diverse paths of migration

Because immigrant youth are extraordinarily diverse, their experiences resist facile generalizations. Nearly 80 percent are youth of color, originating in Latin America, Asia, and the Caribbean. They bring with them an astonishingly wide array of linguistic, religious, and cultural beliefs and practices. Some are the children of highly educated professional parents, and others have parents who are illiterate, low skilled, and struggling in the lowest paid sectors of the service economy.[3] Some families are escaping political, religious, or ethnic persecution; others are lured by the promise of better jobs and the hope for better educational opportunities. Some immigrant youth come to settle permanently; others follow their parents from one migrant work camp to another. Some are documented; others are not. Some engage in transnational strategies, often moving back and forth between their country of birth and their current home in the United States.[4]

Although some immigrant youth come from privileged backgrounds, many suffer from the challenges associated with poverty. Many arrive from poor origins while others experience downward mobility in the process of resettlement. Nearly a quarter of the children of immigrants live below the poverty line, compared to 11 percent of non-Hispanic whites. Nationwide, 37 percent of the children of immigrants report difficulties affording food and they are more than four times as likely as native-born children to live in crowded housing conditions. Children raised in circumstances of socioeconomic deprivation are vulnerable to an array of psychological distresses, including difficulties concentrating and sleeping, anxiety, and depression as well as a heightened propensity for delinquency and violence.[5]

Poverty frequently coexists with a variety of other factors that augment risks, such as single parenthood; residence in neighborhoods plagued with violence, gang activity, and drug trade; and school environments that are segregated, overcrowded, and poorly funded.[6] Many immigrant youth have virtually no direct, systematic, and intimate contact with middle-class white Americans.[7] This segregation affects the kinds of English language encountered by these youth, the quality of schools they will attend, and their access to networks that facilitate entrance into desirable colleges and jobs.

Lost connections and family transitions

By any measure, immigration is one of the most stressful events a family can undergo. Immigrants must learn new cultural expectations and (often) a new language. They are stripped of many of their significant relationships, including family members, friends, and community relations.[8] They also lose the social roles that provided them with culturally scripted notions of how they fit into the world. Without a sense of competence, control, and belonging, many immigrants feel marginalized. These changes in relationships, contexts, and roles are highly disorienting and nearly inevitably lead to a keen sense of loss.[9]

For many new arrivals, the principal motivation for migration is to be reunited with family members who emigrated earlier. For the majority of immigrant youth, the process of family reunification is a long, often painful, and disorienting ordeal. Data derived from the Longitudinal Immigrant Student Adaptation (LISA) study, conducted at the Harvard Graduate School of Education, reveals that 85 percent of the youth underwent separation from one or both parents for periods from six months to more than ten years.[10] Hence, separations are normative to the migratory process. During that time the children are nurtured by other caretakers, to whom they become attached. When a child is called upon to join her parents, although she is happy about the prospect of regaining them, she also loses sustaining contact with her caretaker. After the reunification, youths often find themselves entering new family constellations that include parents who seem like strangers, as well as stepparents, stepsiblings, and siblings they have never met.

Immigrant parents' self-assurance and authority can be undermined both in the outside world and in the more intimate inner world of the family. Through schools, immigrant children typically come into closer contact with American culture than do their parents, who may be removed from American culture, often working in jobs with other immigrants and coethnics.[11] The relative rapidness of the child's absorption into the new culture sometimes creates tensions.[12] Immigrant parents frequently attempt to slow down the process, warning children not to act like other children in the new setting. They may also discipline their children in ways that are accepted in their country of origin but that may conflict with American norms. Because children typically learn English more quickly than their parents do, they often take on new roles as translators and advocates for their families. Culturally scripted family expectations are often challenged by migration.

Once settled in the new land, family members may discover that new obligations and necessities keep them from one another. Many immigrant parents (particularly those coming from poorer backgrounds) work in several jobs. These multiple obligations make them less available to their children than they were prior to migration. Immigrant parents feel that working hard is the best way to help their children, yet these long work hours leave many youth alone. This physical absence compounds the psychological unavailability that often accompanies parental anxiety and depression secondary to migration.[13] Under such circumstances, connections beyond the immediate family may become all the more compelling.

Networks of relationships

Peers, community leaders, adults in schools, church members, and coaches are important in the adaptation of adolescents in general and appear to be particularly important to immigrant adolescents.[14]

These youth are often undergoing profound shifts in their sense of self and are struggling to negotiate changing circumstances in relationships with their parents. These other relationships can provide immigrant youth with compensatory attachments, information about new cultural norms and practices, and tools vital to success in school.

These social relations help immigrant youth and their families in significant ways to navigate the difficult currents and chart a steady course to a better life. They serve a number of functions. Immigrants rely on instrumental social support to provide them with tangible aid (such as running an errand or making a loan) as well as guidance and advice (including information about job and housing leads, cultural expectations in the new context, and the like), which are much needed by disoriented newcomers. Social companionship also serves to maintain and enhance self-esteem, as well as providing acceptance and approval. Quite predictably, a well-functioning social support network is closely linked to better adjustment to the new environment.

For immigrant adolescents, social worlds are also fundamental to the process of identity formation. Their development requires the usual challenges of adolescence complicated by a process of racial and ethnic identification. Indeed, entry into American identities today is by way of a culture of multiculturalism—one experiments, names, and performs identities by creating a hyphenated self. These new identities, crafted in the process of immigrants' uprooting and resettlement, are fluid and multilayered.

This volume

First- and second-generation immigrant youth currently constitute 20 percent of the children growing up in the United States. Thus their healthy development has fundamental long-term implications for our society. As we have seen, immigrant youth undergo a host of changes that can have lasting impacts on their development.

Their journeys follow complex paths—often bifurcating into divergent experiences and varied outcomes. Some youth thrive through immigration; others struggle to cope. It is essential that we deepen our understanding of the factors that influence the development of the burgeoning immigrant youth population.

The present issue of *New Directions for Youth Development* explores in detail some of the major social influences that shape immigrant children's paths in their transition to the United States, and the complex interconnections among those influences. Three of the chapters present data gathered as part of the LISA study. This five-year interdisciplinary and comparative study was directed by Carola Suárez-Orozco and Marcelo Suárez-Orozco and funded by the National Science Foundation, the W.T. Grant Foundation, and the Spencer Foundation. The LISA study for five years followed four hundred immigrant children (ages nine to fourteen at the beginning of the study) who came from five regions (China, Central America, the Dominican Republic, Haiti, and Mexico) to the Boston and San Francisco areas. This interdisciplinary project utilized a variety of methods, including structured student and parent interviews, ethnographic observations, projective and objective measures, reviews of school records and behavior checklists, and teacher questionnaires and interviews. These data provide new glimpses into the world of immigrant youth.

Dario's case study poignantly illustrates the interconnection of multiple social influences on one particular youth's path of migration. The rest of this volume delves into a number of social worlds that can contribute to the positive development of immigrant youth. Our contributing authors also provide insight into who and what are the sources of information about viable identity pathway options. The chapters offer new data on the developmental opportunities and challenges that family roles and responsibilities, school contexts, community organizations, religious involvement and beliefs, gendered expectations, and media influences present to immigrant youth. They also provide insight into the research, practice, and policy implications of these social worlds.

Notes

1. The name used for this case study is a pseudonym; some details have been changed to protect identities. This case study is one of eighty collected by the Harvard Longitudinal Immigrant Student Adaptation study. The ethnographic observations for this case study were conducted by Jeanette Adames; Marcelo Suárez-Orozco and Desiree Qin-Hilliard contributed to the analysis.

2. From "Song of myself," *Leaves of grass.*

3. Suárez-Orozco, M. (2000). "Everything you ever wanted to know about assimilation but were afraid to ask." Daedalus, *129*(4), 1–30.

4. Suárez-Orozco, C., & Suárez-Orozco, M. (2001). *Children of immigration.* Cambridge, MA: Harvard University Press.

5. Capps, R. (2001). *Hardship among children of immigrants: Findings from the 1999 national survey of America's families.* Washington, DC: Urban Institute.

6. Orfield, G., & Yun, J. T. (1999). *Resegregation in American Schools.* Cambridge, MA: Civil Rights Project, Harvard University.

7. Portes, A. (1996). Children of immigrants: Segmented assimilation and its determinants. In A. Portes (Ed.), *The economic sociology of immigration: Essays on networks, ethnicity, and entrepreneurship.* New York: Russell Sage Foundation; Orfield, G. (1995). *Latinos in Education: Recent Trends.* Paper presented to the Harvard Graduate School of Education, Cambridge, MA.

8. Falicov, C. J. (1998). *Latino families in therapy: A guide to multicultural practices.* New York: Guilford Press.

9. Ainslie, R. (1998). Cultural mourning, immigration, and engagement: Vignettes from the Mexican experience. In M. M. Suárez-Orozco (Ed.), *Crossings: Mexican immigration in interdisciplinary perspectives.* Cambridge, MA: David Rockefeller Center for Latin American Studies/Harvard University Press.

10. Suárez-Orozco, C., Todorova, I., & Louie, J. (2002). "Making up for lost time": The experience of separation and reunification among immigrant families. *Family Process, 41*(4), 625–643.

11. Marcelo Suárez-Orozco, "Everything you ever wanted to know," 2000.

12. Falicov, *Latino families,* 1998.

13. Athey, J. L., & Ahearn, F. L. (1991). *Refugee children: Theory, research, and services.* Baltimore, MD: Johns Hopkins University Press.

14. Roffman, J., Suárez-Orozco, C., and Rhodes, J. (forthcoming). Facilitating positive development in immigrant youth: The role of mentors and community organizations. In D. Perkins, L. M. Borden, J. G. Keith, and F. A. Villaruel (Eds.), *Positive youth development: Creating a positive tomorrow.* Brockton, MA: Klewer Press.

CAROLA SUÁREZ-OROZCO *is codirector of the Harvard Immigration Project at the Harvard Graduate School of Education and Scholar in Residence at the Ross Institute in East Hampton, New York.*

IRINA L. G. TODOROVA *is a postdoctoral fellow with the Harvard Immigration Project at the Harvard Graduate School of Education.*

Using survey and observational data, children's contributions to households in a Mexican immigrant community in Chicago are examined. Children provide essential help to their families, including translating, interpreting, and caring for siblings. These daily life activities shape possibilities for learning and development.

2

Responsibilities of children in Latino immigrant homes

Marjorie Faulstich Orellana

RESEARCHERS who study the developmental processes of immigrant youth have generally focused on school achievement and psychosocial outcomes. This body of work has mapped individual pathways of adaptation, acculturation, and achievement, and analyzed broad social trends, by comparing different immigrant groups with one another and with native-born populations.[1] Generally, however, this research does not link outcomes to youths' daily life practices. In ethnographic research on immigrant families,[2] practices have been central but not linked to outcomes, and here children are largely invisible.

NEW DIRECTIONS FOR YOUTH DEVELOPMENT, NO. 100, WINTER 2003 © WILEY PERIODICALS, INC.

Family responsibilities and youth development

Goodnow and Lawrence present a conceptual framework for researchers exploring the work contributions of children to families.[3] They argue that we should think about children's housework as we would think of the housework of any other family member at any stage of the life course and as we would think of any other form of contribution (such as love, money, respect, obedience, or honor). Goodnow and Lawrence thus advocate the use of the term *contribution* rather than *work, job, help*, or *chore*. Further, they call for enriched descriptions of what children do in homes that go beyond the mere quantification of efforts, instead considering *style* (such as mandatory or optional, volunteered or enlisted, taken for granted or reflected upon), the *person-specificity* of tasks (Are tasks shared, substitutable, or fixed? Are they gendered or age-graded?), and the degree of *consensus* that family members hold about their contributions. They argue for examining the impact of various circumstances on the form, nature, and degree of contributions (as well as how changes in any given circumstance alter arrangements), and they list age, gender, competencies, preferences, family positioning, ethnic background, custom, needs, and availability as circumstances that bear consideration. Finally, they suggest that researchers should look closely at the *feelings that people express* about housework in order to understand the significance and role those feelings play in family functioning.

This framework is particularly useful for understanding the relationship between family responsibilities and youth development in immigrant families because it avoids the imposition of both *ethnocentric* norms and *essentialized-culture* norms. It allows for variation in beliefs about what children of different ages and genders are capable of and should be expected to do—variations that are quite marked across cultural groups as well as across time, social contexts, and circumstances.[4] Immigration brings families into contact with other cultures, which may shift their beliefs about children and childhood and dramatically alter the shape of family life (for example, the involvement of adults in the labor force and the location of extended family as supports for childrearing). There may be wider variations in family work patterns among families in immigrant communities than in more settled communities. Studying these variations can provide insights into the processes of immigration, settlement, and cultural change, as well as into "normative" youth development. Patterns may help us understand variations in the achievement and psychosocial development of immigrant youth. Probing the *meanings* that these experiences have for youth and their families is particularly important for understanding developmental outcomes, because the values and beliefs that are taken up in and through these engagements may shape pathways in consequential ways.

Methods

For this exploration of children's contributions to immigrant households I draw from a multimethod program of research on immigrant childhoods developed in several different communities over the last eight years. A prime focus of this work has been on children's contributions to households as translators, language brokers, or what I call *para-phrasers* (a term that invokes a play on the Spanish word *para*, meaning "for") to refer to the purposeful, goal-oriented ways in which children use their knowledge of English to speak and do things *for* others. But in gathering these data we have also learned about children's general involvement in household tasks. I draw from a survey of 280 fifth and sixth graders at a school on the northwest side of Chicago and from observations in the homes of children who were identified as family translators on the basis of their responses to the survey.

I first detail children's responses to the following survey questions:

1. Do you ever translate for other people? (Students who marked yes were queried about *who* they translate for, *what kinds of things* they have translated, and *where* and *how often* they do so.)

2. When you're at home (after school, on weekends, or during vacations), what do you do? (This was followed by a list of options that included "help my family." Those who checked this box were invited to write in a response to the question, What do you help with?)

Next I use field-note data to develop "enriched descriptions" of four children's household responsibilities. I then return to the survey data to consider gendered patterns as well as to link the practice of translating to school achievement, contemplating both positive and negative implications for learning and development.

Range of children's responsibilities in Mexican immigrant homes

Immigrants vary on many dimensions: in their origins (what regions they come from as well as what nation-states), their length of residence in the United States, the nature of the community in which they now live (for instance, one in which they have contact with other coethnics), the degree of contact they have with their home country, and their present and past social class position, among many other factors. These elements may matter a great deal in how parents raise their children here and how children engage in processes of identity construction. Too often, research on immigrants treats groups as an undifferentiated mass and makes little mention of the receiving contexts that shape their experiences in the United States.

The student population at the school where we administered our survey is approximately 75 percent Hispanic and 25 percent white (mostly students of Polish origin), with 90 percent qualifying for free or reduced-price lunches. The Hispanic population (the focus of the research) is mostly from small farming communities in the Mexican states of Guanajuato and Michoacán. Fifty-three percent of the survey respondents are either first- or second-generation immigrants; 24 percent are third-generation and 4 percent are fourth-generation. Most of the foreign-born and first-generation children in this neighborhood immigrated with their families soon after their birth; thus they constitute part of the "1.5 generation"[5] and share many characteristics with their second-generation peers who were born in the United States of immigrant parents. Many families own their own houses (duplexes that are often shared with extended family or rented out to fellow immigrants); many have lived in this neighborhood for more than ten years, often after living elsewhere in the city. Thus this is a somewhat settled immigrant community, in contrast with the highly transient "first stop" community I studied in Los Angeles.[6]

Quantifying household tasks

The survey data paint a broadly stroked portrait of children's household responsibilities in this community. Sixty-four percent of these fifth and sixth graders indicated that they help their families. In their write-in responses, twenty-three students framed their contributions as "chores," three used the Spanish term *quehaceres* ("things to do"), five said they help with "everything," and others named specific activities, especially cleaning (55 percent) but also cooking (9 percent), washing dishes (5 percent), and caring for siblings or cousins (8 percent). The majority—83 percent—answered yes to the question, Do you ever translate for other people? Sixty-six percent said they translate for their mothers at least sometimes, 51 percent said they translate for their fathers at least sometimes, and 32 percent said they translate for their younger siblings at least sometimes.

It is important to recognize, however, that these are self-reported answers to a preformulated question requiring a write-in response. The survey likely elicited what students assumed to be appropriate ways for naming the help they provide at home, or what was salient to them about their household work. Although only eight children indicated that they help with child care, we know from observations at the school and from home observations that many of these fifth and sixth graders walk younger siblings to and from school. Indeed, most of our case study participants provide at least some degree of sibling care. Further, although only two respondents spontaneously reported that they help their families by translating, when queried directly earlier in the same survey, the majority indicated that they did so. This suggests that some activities, such as translating and sibling care, may be invisible or taken-for-granted forms of household work, not ones that occur to youth when asked the general question of how they help their families. Our observations indicate that many translations take place spontaneously and are woven into the fabric of everyday life. Observations further suggest that youth in this community may be much more involved in household work than survey responses indicate—though with considerable variation across families.

Following Goodnow and Lawrence's suggestions, I want to move beyond the mere quantification of contributions. I draw now from extensive field notes recorded by team members based on observations in the homes of case study participants. Vignettes of these youth help to illustrate variations in involvement, as shaped by family constellations, parents' work responsibilities and schedules, and individual characteristics. (All names are pseudonyms, selected by the participants.)

Brianna

Twelve-year-old Brianna lives with her mother, father, ten-year-old brother, and four-year-old sister on the second floor of a two-flat building. Her parents immigrated from Guerrero, Mexico, a few years before Brianna was born. Like most of the youth in our study, she has a rich network of extended family living nearby.

Also like many of the families in our study, Brianna's parents have arranged their work schedules so they can be home for their children; they work alternating shifts in the same factory. There is a brief overlap period between the time her mother leaves for work and the time her father gets home, however, creating a need for Brianna's involvement; she walks her brother home from school and is responsible for her siblings during that time. Brianna's mother usually leaves food prepared for the family (there is no expectation that her father will do so), but Brianna sometimes helps prepare meals; she also does the laundry, ironing, and cleaning around the house. Her father pays her $5 to $7 a week, with the expectation that she will do "something" every day. Brianna uses the money to buy clothes, magazines, and school supplies.

Brianna's family responsibilities, including translating for her mother and grandmother, take place in the sphere of everyday life and extended family relations. They resonate in many ways with those of three other eldest daughters in our study, each of whom has younger siblings and each of whom takes on considerable household tasks. The other girls, however, are not paid for these contributions; they are simply expected to help. They might be given spending money from time to time, but this is not considered payment for chores, nor is it explicitly named an allowance.

Josh

Twelve-year-old Josh is also the oldest in his family, but with only one sister who is close in age. He lives in a house with many adults (his mother, father, aunt, uncle, and two adult cousins), whose presence seems to diminish the need for Josh or his sister to take on household work such as cleaning or cooking. Because none of these adults are fluent in English, however, the children are often called to serve as translators. Josh is active in answering phone calls, delivering messages, and coordinating information among family members.

Josh's father works in a hotel. Until recently, Josh's mother did not work, but she now has a second-shift job in a chicken-processing plant. Like Brianna's mother, and other working mothers in our study whose husbands are home for the dinner hour, Josh's mother prepares food for the family before leaving for work each day. Josh's aunt is expected to be responsible for the children when both parents are working, but Josh's mother does not find her sister to be reliable. She contrasts life here with life in Mexico: "There, there are always the grandparents to care for the grandchildren." She notes further that "and here you have to pay even family."

Josh indicated on his survey that he helps his family by doing undefined "chores." We did not directly observe Josh as he engaged in what we might consider chores, and his mother and aunt take care of the basic cooking, shopping, and cleaning requirements of the household. Josh does help to maintain the family computer, and he translates when his English skills are needed. He also sometimes accompanies his father to work, where he assists him in setting up banquet halls. When Josh is home he avidly plays video games and watches the news on CNN.

Jessica

Thirteen-year-old Jessica is not the oldest in her family; her brother is two years older. Her mother is also expecting a new baby. She lives with her family on the third floor of a three-flat building that her uncle owns. Jessica and her brother were born in Mexico and immigrated to the United States with their parents when they were toddlers.

Jessica's parents both work, but her mother is planning to stop when the baby is born. Jessica is expected to help with housework, especially during the summers. These days Jessica generally spends an hour or two straightening or cleaning her own room, the living room, the bathroom, and the kitchen. She washes dishes, sweeps and mops the floor, and cleans the table. Jessica told us that her brother is actually expected to tidy up the living room, because that is where he sleeps—she noted somewhat matter-of-factly that this is his only chore—but because he doesn't usually do this, she does it for him.

Jessica is gearing up for more home responsibilities when her baby brother is born. Her mother is teaching her how to cook and Jessica is writing down the instructions so she will be able to cook when her mother is taking care of the baby. Jessica anticipates that she will also help with diapers, washing the baby's bottles, and doing laundry. When we asked her how she feels about these responsibilities, she said, "Well, I mean sometimes I think about like it's good for my mom, she has to rest a little bit, and I think I'm going to do all right." At the same time, she displayed some ambivalence: "I have to stop doing my things to help her, but sometimes I mean I'm like helping her so it doesn't bother [me]."

Monique

Twelve-year-old Monique is an only child, born to teenage parents soon after they emigrated from Durango, Mexico, to Chicago. Monique's parents own their apartment building; they live on the second floor and rent the first floor to another family. Monique's uncle and aunt live in the basement.

Monique's responsibilities at home, like Josh's, seem to be minimal. Her parents work at the same factory, on different shifts. Again, like other mothers in our study, Monique's mother tidies the apartment and makes supper before leaving for work each day. Monique does not talk about cleaning or chores when we ask her about her daily life, and on the survey she does not indicate that she helps her family. When her parents are working and she is not in school, she stays home alone and watches television or listens to music; she is not allowed to leave the house during those times. She complains of being bored. About translating, Monique notes, "I translate for my mom, mostly about bills." She adds that it can be boring, but she doesn't mind it too much because "you help people."

Gender and family positioning

Across these cases we find variations in the extent, nature, distribution, and meanings of household work. These variations seem to be at least partly shaped by positioning in the family, with older children taking on more responsibilities, especially vis-à-vis younger siblings; and by gender, with girls generally assuming more responsibility for traditionally female work such as cleaning and providing child care than do boys. The gender comparison is clearest in families like those of Josh and Jessica, because each has a sibling of the opposite gender that is close in age. In these families, the girls are not the eldest, but they take on more household responsibilities than do their brothers, especially for cleaning.

The gendered distribution of household chores is also revealed in our survey data. Seventy-one percent of the girls said they help their families, compared to 58 percent of the boys ($p < .03$). When we look at the specific subcategory of "cleaning" (based on students' write-in responses), we find that 63 percent of all girls said they help by cleaning, compared to 37 percent of all boys ($p < .04$).

Beliefs and practices shaped by needs

Although beliefs about what boys and girls of different ages are capable of, or should be expected to do, may shape the distribution of household tasks, the practices that are actually enacted are influenced by parents' needs and by the availability of other help. In Josh's family, for example, there was little need for Josh *or* his sister to take on certain tasks because of the presence of many adults. In Monique's family there was little need because of the absence of younger children. Working parents with young children at home may rely more heavily on their oldest children, especially for child care, and girls in these homes may disproportionately meet the household work needs that are created when both parents work or when a new baby is born. The abilities or perceived abilities of children may also weigh in, but perceptions of abilities are in turn influenced by dispositions. Josh's father, for example, believes that Josh's sister Marcia is the better translator of the two and so calls on Marcia to help more often than on Josh. We saw little evidence to suggest that Marcia is actually more skilled at translating than Josh, but as with Jessica, it did appear that she was more willing to help than was her brother.

Even when practices are not overtly attached to beliefs about gender, they may become gendered because the nature of family relationships has a strong gender component. This was clear in Jessica's case; as she noted, she spends more time with her mother than her brother does, and thus translates more often than he does.

As girls grow into adolescence, this may result in particular tensions; several of the mothers made comments such as "ella ya no me quiere ayudar" (she doesn't want to help me any more) when their daughters expressed reluctance to translate for them.

Positive and negative implications for development

Tensions between mothers and daughters over dispositions toward helping may be an indicator of what Suárez-Orozco and Suárez-Orozco call gender and generational "role dissonance."[7] Jessica's mother believes that a proper daughter should want to help her mother in any way she can, including by using her English skills to benefit the family. From a "mainstream" developmental perspective, children's involvement in household work, especially as translators, may be considered problematic: it places too many demands on them, takes time from their studies, and gives them responsibilities that children should not have. From the families' standpoint, however, children's involvement in household work may be considered essential for their overall "educación,"[8] facilitating their moral, social, and civic development. From an emic perspective, then, generational role dissonance occurs not when children translate for their families but when they do not do so when asked. Many developmental researchers assume the opposite—that children's speaking for adults constitutes a form of role reversal that can undermine parental authority.[9]

"It's just normal"

In our home observations we found little evidence that children feel burdened either by translation responsibilities or by general household work. Kids talked about translating as something that was "just normal" or "just something they do," and most of the translation activities we documented (through children's self-reports in

journal entries, in their responses to the survey, and through obser-
vation) were everyday sorts of activities: the translation of daily
mail, phone calls, conversations, television shows, or "on the
street." The potentially burdensome sorts of translation situations
that have received considerable attention in the popular press, such
as translating for doctors and lawyers,[10] seem to be relatively
unusual occurrences. Similarly, for the most part the children did
not call their household responsibilities chores or work, but simply part of daily life. When asked directly about this work, they
might complain or make sibling comparisons; but we saw no evidence that housework interfered with their studies or that it elim-
inated time for recreational activities. As Monique hinted, helping
may be "boring," but it's better than being bored without having
helped anyone.

Academic payoffs

Our interest in how practices tie to outcomes led us to ask whether
translating experiences may facilitate not just children's social and
moral development but also their academic skills. Observations of
the youth suggest that this might be so; translating involves sophisticated bilingual capacities, literacy skills (as children translate
many genres of the printed word from a variety of real-world
domains), and real-world math abilities (as kids help with everyday math practices such as paying bills, writing checks, opening
bank accounts, and making purchases). Translators potentially
develop the ability to reflect on language and cultural practices.
Jasmine's mother saw it this way: "When she talks with people it's
as if she grows more."

Thus we designed ways to link outcome measures to children's
reported daily life translation experiences through statistical analyses of the survey data. Indeed, we found that the children in our
study who were identified as active translators for their families
(using a composite variable based on their responses to all of the
survey questions regarding translation) did significantly better on

standardized tests of reading and math achievement in sixth grade than did their nontranslator peers, even when controlling for early school achievement.

Scaffolding for enhanced learning opportunities

How translating and other household tasks are viewed and treated, however, greatly shapes the learning opportunities they provide. In some observed situations, children worked without support, and their parents did not seem to appreciate their skills or the challenges they faced. In other situations, children were supported in their efforts and their contributions were both valued and validated. In these cases, translating may offer prime opportunities for learning. As Miguel's mother explained, "I believe [translating] helps him because he learns from this. Because if he didn't . . . have to translate to anyone then I think he would only talk in English. . . . Words that he doesn't know how to tell me in Spanish I also try to help with what they mean. So he learns what they mean."

General household work such as cleaning and child care may have less direct or obvious payoffs than does translating, and to the extent that engagement in these practices keeps children from academic pursuits it may diminish rather than enhance their intellectual growth. However, as I have argued elsewhere,[11] the dispositions toward helpfulness that children in our study expressed can be applied to school learning activities if they are given the opportunity to do so.

Research, practices, and policy implications

I have used both survey and observational data to examine children's contributions to households in an immigrant community. The survey data allow us to identify the broad contours of children's work as well as gendered dimensions of these experiences, and to systematically link practices to outcomes. The observations facilitate a deeper and more nuanced consideration of the circumstances and meanings of household work, as well as of the relationships within which this work takes place.

These analyses reveal that children in this community take on significant amounts of household responsibility, but there is considerable variation across families. How children's involvement in household tasks compares with that of youth in other communities bears further research. This can be done by comparing the amount of time spent on housework by children of different ages and genders in different locales; but to grasp the role that household work plays in youth development in situations of cultural change, it is important as well to understand what children and families see to be too little, too much, or normal.

We also need studies that can take into account the varied and changing circumstances of immigrant families' lives. All families' needs change over the course of the life span—especially as children grow up and others are born—but immigrant families may change in additional ways, as they acquire English, learn about cultural and institutional practices, become citizens, and change employment. Immigrants are particularly vulnerable to shifting labor market trends and global sociopolitical conditions, and shifts in adult employment patterns may mean changes in children's household contributions.

Knowing more about how children participate in family life is important for forging culturally responsive policies and practices. For example, recognizing older siblings' caregiving responsibilities and bilingual youths' translating skills can help us imagine new ways that children can be translators, teachers, and tutors to others. Instead of seeing these responsibilities as problems, we can see them as *opportunities*—opportunities that resonate with families' cultural values even as they pave the way for new possibilities for immigrant youth.

Notes

1. Rumbaut, R. G., & Portes, A. (2001). *Ethnicities: Children of immigrants in America.* New York: Russell Sage Foundation; Coll, C. G., & Magnuson, K. (1997). The psychological experience of immigration: A developmental perspective. In A. Booth, A. Crouter, & N. Landale (Eds.), *International migration and family change: The experience of U.S. immigrants.* Mahway, NJ: Erlbaum; Suárez-Orozco, C., & Suárez-Orozco, M. M. (2001). *Children of immigration.* Cambridge, MA: Harvard University Press.

2. Hondagneu-Sotelo, P. (1994). *Gendered transitions: Mexican experiences of immigration.* Berkeley: University of California Press; Kibria, N. (1993). *Family tightrope: The changing lives of Vietnamese Americans.* Princeton, NJ: Princeton University Press.

3. Goodnow, J. J., & Lawrence, J. Work contributions to the family: Developing a conceptual and research framework. In A. J. Fuligni (Ed.), *Family obligation and assistance during adolescence: Contextual variations and developmental implications.* San Francisco: Jossey-Bass.

4. Rogoff, B. (2003). *The cultural nature of human development.* New York: Oxford University Press.

5. Portes, A. (Ed.) (1996). *The New Second Generation.* New York: Sage.

6. Orellana, M. F. (2001, Fall). The work kids do: Mexican and Central American immigrant children's contributions to households and schools in California. *Harvard Educational Review,* 366–389.

7. Suárez-Orozco & Suárez-Orozco (2001).

8. Reese, L., Gallimore, R., Goldenberg, C., & Balzano, S. (1995). "Immigrant Latino parents' future orientations for their children." In R. F. Macias & R. G. García Ramos (Eds.), *Changing schools for changing students: An anthology of research on language minorities, schools, and society.* Santa Barbara: University of California Linguistic Minority Research Institute.

9. Coll & Magnuson (1997). Athey, J. L., and Ahearn, F. L. (Eds.) (1991). *Refugee children: Theory, research, and services.* Baltimore: Johns Hopkins University Press; Baptiste, D. A. (1993). Immigrant families, adolescents, and acculturation: Insights for therapists. *Marriage and Family Review,* 19, 341–363; Buriel, R. W., and DeMent, T. L. (1997). Immigration and sociocultural change in Mexican, Chinese, and Vietnamese American families. In A. Booth, A. Crouter, & N. Landale (Eds.), *Immigration and the family: Research and policy on U.S. immigrants.* Mahwah, NJ: Erlbaum.

10. Gold, M. (1999, May 24). Small voice for her parents. *Los Angeles Times,* A1; Flores, V. (1993, April 4). Language skills translate to major duties for kids. *Chicago Sun-Times,* 4; Wallace, D. (2002, February 15). Bilingual teens may do translating. *Chicago Daily Herald,* 1.

11. Orellana (2001).

MARJORIE FAULSTICH ORELLANA *is associate professor at the Graduate School of Education at the University of California, Los Angeles.*

Vietnamese students must contend with the burden of the myth of being a model minority. As a result of adults' high expectations of them, Vietnamese youth receive structural and ideological advantages over other nonwhite racial groups. Further, the students themselves reinforce the model minority image as they attempt to attain educational mobility. The authors examine the role of two distinct school contexts within the same school that shape the academic outcomes of Vietnamese students contending with the pressures of being considered members of the model minority.

3

Surfing the "model minority" wave of success: How the school context shapes distinct experiences among Vietnamese youth

Gilberto Q. Conchas, Cristina C. Pérez

I think it's just not that there are really smart Asian people out there, it is the standards that they have set up for Asian people. . . . They are really high and working up to them is so hard. . . . We just make the best of what we have. . . . I know that there are Asian kids now that are really bad, that they don't do anything. I mean, it's all a stereotype.

—Diana, high school junior

NEW DIRECTIONS FOR YOUTH DEVELOPMENT, NO. 100, WINTER 2003 © WILEY PERIODICALS, INC.

IN CONTEMPORARY U.S. society and culture, Asians are depicted as "model minorities." They are portrayed as fully integrated members of society who have overcome ideological and structural discrimination in education and in the workforce.[1] Current research, for instance, indicates that Asians consistently outperform youth of other races and ethnicities throughout U.S. schools, despite social and economic inequality.[2] Recently there have been discussions that contest the usefulness of the model minority stereotype, challenging the model minority representation as a harmful characterization. The model minority stereotype, nonetheless, is the dominant folk model of Asian American school performance and social mobility.

Three major theoretical perspectives guide our understanding of the educational attainments of Asian American students in U.S. schools. The first framework suggests that Asian culture promotes education. Scholars have shown that Asians possess traits that are highly regarded by the dominant group: hard work, motivation, respect, and the delay of gratification for future success.[3] Asian families and parents in particular aid in this process by socializing "their children to work hard in school in order to uphold the family honor."[4] This cultural paradigm, however, does not fully clarify the variations in Asian American student outcomes.

The perspective of relative functionalism, on the other hand, argues that the educational attainment of Asians is highly influenced by the opportunity structures associated with social mobility and cannot be attributed solely to cultural factors.[5] While cultural values play a role, relative functionalists find that the "Asian American preoccupation with education is primarily an environmentally induced reaction to survival in a hostile society."[6] Hence, "education is increasingly functional as a means to mobility when other avenues are blocked."[7] The question remains as to why some Asians perform well in school and others do not.

Finally, the cultural ecological paradigm endeavors to explain the relationship between minority status, perceptions of the limited opportunity structure, and academic achievement. Scholars distinguish between "voluntary minorities"—those immigrants who freely chose to immigrate to this country in order to improve their lives (such as Asians)—and "involuntary minorities"—those forced into the United States through slavery (such as African Americans) or conquest (such as Mexicans and Pacific Islanders).[8] According to cultural ecologists, differences in academic achievement result from a racial group's perceptions of opportunity structures and their consequent interpretations and reactions to schooling. Voluntary minorities do well in school because they foresee upward mobility, whereas, involuntary minorities resist the notion that school will lead to social and economic mobility. The cultural ecological framework also reinforces the model minority stereotype[9] and characterizes Asians as a monolithic entity devoid of within-group variations.[10]

In this chapter we develop a more comprehensive understanding of Asian American success by exploring the social and academic experiences of immigrant and native-born Vietnamese high school students. While Vietnamese students constitute the largest recently emigrated Asian ethnic group,[11] few studies have closely examined their experiences in schooling. Vietnamese students make for an interesting case due to the bimodal nature of their outcomes and the reality that they do not have the educational advantages of other Asian groups, such as Koreans, Japanese, or Chinese. In this study, therefore, we specifically examine and challenge the model minority stereotype's usefulness in helping to understand patterns of academic identity and ability among high-achieving Vietnamese students in distinct school contexts.

Methods and setting

To facilitate our understanding of the cultural and structural processes that make school success possible for some racial minority youth, this study compares Vietnamese students' experiences in two academic programs.[12] Rich data collected in interviews, focus groups, and observations with twenty-seven Vietnamese students of Chinese descent in the tenth through twelfth grades (seventeen immigrant and ten U.S.-born) capture a multiplicity of student voices. Sixteen boys and eleven girls compose the sample. Two years were spent observing the day-to-day student-student and student-teacher interactions, interviewing students and teachers, mapping seating arrangements, and collecting site documents. Teacher and administrator interviews augment the sample by providing adult perceptions of Vietnamese youth and an opportunity to discuss how students' subsequent reactions reflect or challenge these perceptions. Close attention is also paid to the entire school culture, but interviews and observations concentrated on the school's attempt to promote success.

Baldwin High School is located in a predominantly racial minority community in an urban area in California. It is one of several comprehensive high schools serving a low-income and racially diverse student body that reflects the larger community. During the period of 1996–1998, Baldwin High educated approximately eighteen hundred students from more than a dozen countries, speaking a multiplicity of languages. African Americans represented 65 percent, Asians 20 percent, Latinos 10 percent, whites 4 percent, and Filipinos and Native Americans 1 percent. Baldwin High encompassed a substantial Asian American population as well: 92 percent were Vietnamese students of Chinese descent, Filipinos accounted for 7 percent, and Pacific Islanders, 1 percent.

Baldwin offered a full curriculum ranging from general classes to advanced placement. The high school housed several career academies for students interested in pursuing specific careers that required postsecondary to graduate degrees, and a well-established advanced placement (AP) program. The AP program served only sixty-six students: 50 percent Asian American, 33 percent African American, 9 percent white, and 8 percent Latino. The courses in the AP program set rigorous standards in reading, writing, and discussion. AP classes were offered to students in the tenth through twelfth grades in the humanities and social sciences. The students in this program formed a very small and exclusive network of high achievers who became separated from the rest of the student body. Although teachers, students, and administrators viewed these students as the most academically talented, data exposed high levels of alienation and depression within the program. The culture of the program stressed individualism and high levels of competition.

The Medical Academy, a school-within-a-school program, began as a dropout prevention initiative in 1985. Since its inception, it has recruited students with high potential who are interested in health and bioscience careers. Fundamental to the Medical Academy's educational philosophy is the notion that all students, whether low-achieving or high-achieving, must enroll in higher education. The racial and ethnic makeup of the Medical Academy closely resembled the racial composition of the entire school. This study concentrates on the Vietnamese students enrolled in the Medical Academy and the AP program.

Vietnamese origin students at Baldwin High School

> [My parents] were each born and raised in a very poor family in Vietnam. Therefore, they didn't have a chance to complete school or get the education that they wanted. My parents had a lot of dreams and goals that they wanted to accomplish, but these dreams disappeared once school was not part of their life. They were poor and could not afford schooling. All they had to look forward to was working on the rice and plant fields, a daily routine in their lives back home.
> —Kim, high school senior

Kim's story reflects the experiences of the majority of Vietnamese students at Baldwin High. All of the students in the sample came from low-socioeconomic-status (SES) backgrounds. Their parents were not the highly educated Vietnamese who immigrated prior to 1965. On the contrary, this cohort is part of the post-1965 refugees (or their sons and daughters) commonly referred to as the "boat people."[13] Many of these youth hailed from families that worked farms in their native Vietnam and, due to lack of skills in demand in the urban American centers where they settled, found themselves relegated to low-income status. If they found work, it was in the service industry as cooks, seamstresses or tailors, and manicurists. If not, they remained unemployed and on welfare. Many families struggled with alcoholism, violence, single-parent or no parent families, burdensome medical and psychological conditions, and children at high risk of dropping out of school.

In many instances, students served as their parents' liaisons to the harsh realities of U.S. society as they adapted, sometimes slowly and painfully, to their new surroundings. Forced to cope with the many social and economic problems that political refugee families experienced, the students hesitantly lamented their predicament behind closed doors. Steven, a senior, demonstrated his resiliency in managing a difficult home and school life as he recounted with emotion:

I acted as translator for doctors, employers, [and] cashiers. I made sure bills were paid on time and the household matters were taken care of. I planned a schedule for all daily duties. Some of them, when added to my school day, gave me a fifteen or sixteen hour day. As I entered my sophomore year in high school my mother developed diabetes and I had to see to her medical care, including her phobia of doctors and needles. At about the same time, my father slipped into a deep depression. For two years, I managed to keep them healthy and alive. . . . I felt crushed by [the] enormous weight of responsibility.

These were difficult burdens to place on a teenager who was also negotiating between the social and cultural demands in the home and those in his new host society. Nevertheless, a significant number of Vietnamese students achieved academic excellence, despite difficult structural, historical, and cultural experiences.

Most Vietnamese students self-identified as first- and second-generation immigrants to the United States. They came from families that had little formal education in their home country. Vietnamese parents lacked familiarity with the American educational system but sought to capitalize on this new opportunity to educate their children. Students reported that their parents pushed them to excel in school so they could achieve better positions and a higher economic status than their parents. Vietnamese parents made it obvious that they wanted their children to graduate from high school and attend college. Their parents constantly reminded them of the sacrifices they made so their children would have prospects they never enjoyed in their homeland.

The students struggled to meet these demands placed upon them, but they also felt the impact of their economic and racial identities as poor Southeast Asians. Vietnamese students had to cope with an often hostile racial and ethnic climate in school. Fred explained that, to him, "money and race are definitely an obstacle . . . but there's also racial tension in the real world." Similarly, Alex reported that his "racial background is a very big issue because you can never get rid of racism. . . . There are people's minds out there that you can't change . . . and you will need a lot of money to get yourself through school and if you are poor . . . it will be hard too." To Alex, his college and career expectations appeared to be intricately linked with his economic and racial identities.

One English teacher commented, "[C]ertain African American kids . . . provide the worst stereotypes about Asians and conversely there are lots of stereotypes among Asian kids toward African Americans." In the general and advanced placement programs, teachers as well as students remained racially and ethnically divided. In the larger school, racial separation was most visible within the low-tracked courses, at lunch, and during social activities. Students generally separated themselves based on race (and gender). Regrettably, racial tension and violence permeated the daily lives of many Asian students at Baldwin. Students report that black youths "picked" on them because they perceived them as nerds and weak.

Rather than mitigate the friction, the teaching and classroom environment exacerbated the racial climate. White and Asian teachers generally taught white and Asian students, whereas black teachers predominantly taught black and Latino youth. The African American instructors blamed the counselors for the racial segregation, while some white and Asian faculty complained that African American teachers disregarded Asian students' hard work and did not want them in their classes. One white male math teacher stated, "there's a lot of racism in the faculty here. . . . I essentially think it's some of the African American teachers that really don't want to acknowledge the Asian kids." Interestingly, school structures and cultures reflected the racial politics of society at large. Intergroup relations, however, differed among the distinct school contexts. How students responded to race relations depended on their academic program.

Academic identity groups

Two distinct high-achieving Vietnamese academic communities, which self-identified as the *Dedicators* and the *Team Players*, with unique ways of viewing their schooling experiences existed at Baldwin. Differences in experiences resulted from academic structures and cultural processes within the school that shaped distinct student ideologies that either reflected the status quo or challenged it. Whether they contested or reflected this image, students retained several key characterizations of it as descriptive markers in their relationships with students from other races and ethnicities at Baldwin High.

Vietnamese within the AP program comprised the highest-achieving Asian Americans at Baldwin High, with an average 3.5 GPA. They tended to identify themselves as Dedicators because they were industrious workers, dedicated to school. They were academically challenged in higher-level critical thinking courses and had solid goals and experience for attaining social mobility. These students were competitive with one another and felt superior to other students. Star, a Graphics Academy and AP student, describes "this little sense and little air of superiority" resulting from their elevated status at Baldwin High. Star and others in the program felt strongly about their hard work ethic and their persistence in achieving high academic standing.

Asian American students in the Medical Academy also maintained a strong academic record, with an average GPA of 3.2. The Team Players were a community of students who worked well with one another, had a common purpose to do well in school, and created a healthy and safe learning environment that included non-Vietnamese peers. Unlike the Dedicators, the Team Players had been exposed to racially diverse schooling. As they made friends with students from other backgrounds, they overcame racial insecurities and stereotypes by relating to other students as individuals. Team Players often voiced sophisticated interpretations and reactions to the perceived success of their racial group as they contemplated their minority status in school. Although critical of characterizations of Asian Americans as success stories, they too, like the Dedicators, benefited from the model minority construct.

The Dedicators' personal assessments reflected the model minority characterizations espoused by the media, scholars, peers, and teachers. These students attributed their academic success to their home environment and regarded their parents as instrumental in motivating them toward academic success. They believed that their families raised them to be high achievers. For instance, Stacey recalls how "from childhood, we were brought up to do well in school, and it just continues on here." Daisy, a classmate, explained that Vietnamese parents "just expect it" and "the looks they give you" are enough to show what they demanded from her. "You know, it is a disgrace if you don't do well."

The pressure to do well, intensified by far-reaching consequences for failure, permeated the Vietnamese students' daily life. To them, the family's honor was at stake. If they did not achieve high marks, they feared they would disgrace the family. The students knew about the difficult journey their parents had made from Vietnam to America and understood their family's difficult economic situation. Many students internalized these sacrifices. They assumed an obligation to uplift the entire family's social and economic well-being.[14] Nguyen, a senior, described it this way: "Life for my parents was very hard when they came to America. Without any education, the only jobs they could find were waitressing and delivering newspapers. When they had me and my brothers and my sisters, their hopes and dreams were to see us succeed in life. They did not want us to suffer through life like they had. They wanted this so badly that they did not realize that putting pressure on me was hurting me more instead of helping me."

The Team Players shared with the Dedicators a belief that strong family expectations and support shaped and mediated their high academic standards. Every Vietnamese student cited family background as fundamental for academic success. These students surmised that their parents were stern and expected more of them than did the parents of non-Asian students. Fred, for example, conjectured that "many times, Asian families tend to be more strict and

they expect . . . the child to study hard, work hard, go to college."
Similarly, Shelley explains how her "family has been pushing a lot
about education. . . . When [she] slacks off . . . they tell [her] to do
this and do that." The Vietnamese parents enforced the students'
schooling demands and did not allow them to slack. The students
understood that their parents resolutely placed their hopes of success on them.

While the Team Players acknowledged the high rates of academic success among Asians, they also recognized that despite
strong family support, not all Asian students did well. They dis-
credited the notion that all Asians were high achievers. Genie, for
instance, dismissed the Asian image of success as just a "stereotype
. . . like some Asians are good in math and English and many are
not." It was a major misrepresentation, according to many Team
players, to label all Asian students as smart and high achievers.
They reported that many of their peers cut class, smoked, abused
alcohol and drugs, became teenage parents, and joined youth gangs.
Fred pointed to the exploding number of Asian youth gangs in the
greater Bay Area, reporting, "San Francisco has two hundred Asian
gangs in Chinatown and Oakland has about thirty." Hence, these
students considered it unfair to categorize all Asians as high achievers, recognizing that many needed additional educational assistance.

Structuring competition versus collaborative learning

While the Medical Academy fostered a climate of healthy collaboration, the AP program engendered intense competition. Although
the AP Vietnamese students reported feeling part of an academic
community, divisions endured. Their community was fragmented
into what students termed "inner circles." For Daisy, inner circles
were "sort of little communities within" the larger programs. Interestingly, students formed inner circles on the basis of academic status. In an interview, Star explained how inner circles were formed:
"Well, it depends on if you're an ego person actually . . . on how
well you do in school." Similarly, Sang described "invisible" divisions made by the students themselves in these programs, based on

who does well academically and who does not: "Good students always hang around with good students. It gets to form an invisible line." Students wanted desperately to belong to one of the inner circles and continuously had to prove that they were worthy of being part of the "in crowd."

Students faced tremendous academic competition, and some, like Stacey, viewed the rivalry as envy: "Um, there is so much jealousy." Most of these students strove to live up to the model minority image of high academic achievers. Simply, these students, as Daisy described, just "want to do better and shine." They wanted the recognition that academic superiority brings, not only from other students and their family, but from the teachers as well. They were conscious of teachers' perceptions of them and they did not want to change the positive images of them as model students.

Some students in the AP program revealed the personal costs of the highly encouraged and seemingly innocuous academic competition. They reported that these pressures led to emotional instability, such as low self-esteem, depression, and anxiety. Health-related consequences of academic and social anxieties were not infrequent.

The Team Players, on the other hand, included a group of students who worked well with one another and who had begun to build a strong sense of community. They spoke of feelings of inclusion based on relationships and high levels of camaraderie. They felt they belonged to an extended family kinship in the school. Many perceived their peers as "brothers" and "sisters." "It can be like a family," Sandy said. They recognized the importance of collaboration—not only for their social well-being, but also for school success.

The structural initiation of teamwork among Medical Academy students helped reduce competition and increase racial tolerance. Sandy, for instance, reported how students actually praised one another "when they get the right answer." She cheerfully commented, "I'd be, like, you go!" Team Players believed they were less competitive because they had a common goal. Kevin said that in the Medical Academy "you know what direction you wanna go, you want to get in the health profession, and so then you focus on that with the other students and we help each other."

Although Team Players preferred to work with their own ethnic group, the less competitive and more integrated setting facil-
itated the creation of a healthy social and racial climate. Kim
noted that her experiences led to a greater level of racial bonding
among the students: "We still work with other Asians a lot, but
you work with each other no matter what. . . . It's like, if your
teacher wants you to, you get to know each other, like socialize,
so I guess doing a project or research makes you, like . . . , the
stereotype that you thought about blacks at first changed." Similarly, Alex reported that he tends to work and "sit with his Asian
friends in the academy. . . . But I know blacks and Latinos too."
Racial integration helped build relationships across groups and
decreased social and academic tension. At the same time, it led
students to be more critical of the model minority typology. What
does this all mean?

Social perceptions as ideological and structural enhancements

The model minority stereotype socially and academically advantaged Asian students at Baldwin High. Both groups of Vietnamese
students attributed their success to their cultural and parental
socialization and adult perceptions of them as model students. Students were advantaged ideologically and structurally through teachers' high expectations. Ideologically, teachers' high expectations
reinforced students' high motivation and self-esteem. Structurally,
these higher expectations meant that students were enrolled in the
more advanced classes.

Vietnamese students benefited from adults' favorable perception
of Asian students at Baldwin High. Interviews with teachers,
administrators, and counselors signaled a significant tendency
among the educators to view Asian students as focused, enthusiastic, and prepared to do work. Educators commented on the dis-
parate inspiration levels between Asians and other racial ethnic
groups; they viewed African Americans and Latinos as lazy and less

academically motivated. One white female teacher, for example, concluded that Asian students "are . . . the most motivated in this school and anyone here knows that. . . . African Americans and the . . . Hispanics and Latinos are kind of split between who are the least motivated."

Students commented that teachers expected great things from them simply because of their ethnic identity. "Teachers look at appearance and just because we are a certain thing, they expect us to do good all the time." These higher expectations elevated Asian students as superior learners while simultaneously placing greater stress on them. In turn, Asian students attempted to actualize these expectations. They did not want to let down their teachers, parents, or community. The following dialogue with two students illuminates their responses to teacher expectations:

CONCHAS: Do teachers have the same expectations of all students?
LISA: Not always. . . . People around you, they just don't see us different, like teachers just assume that we are all the same . . . that means that us, Asian people, have to set a higher standard, since you want to live up to what they . . . are calling you or what they assume that you are.
CONCHAS: So you think that Asians are stereotyped in different ways?
KIM: Okay, it's like they treat us in some different ways because we are Asian. We are suppose to be smart, so they, they want you to be smart in some ways and they think that you *are* smart by looking at you. . . . All they want to see is the stereotype.

The students believed that the majority of teachers based their expectations of Asian students on stereotypes of Asian achievement.

Teacher and counselor perceptions of Asians as model minorities assisted these youth in accessing the most prestigious academic programs. Key staff members' high expectations of Asian students mediated the tracking of these students into highly regarded college-bound programs, resulting in racial and ethnic divisions. Minority status was thought to be a strong link to academic success: "[t]he teachers in [AP] are Asian and white . . . and they tend to choose

Asian and white students." Data suggest a strong association between ideological and structural factors in assessing Asian students' access to higher-level programs.

Discussion and policy implications

Cultural ecologists argue that immigrant minorities, as opposed to involuntary ones, interpret and react to schooling positively in order to attain social mobility.[15] Immigrants evaluate their current situation in the United States in reference to their former situation in their country of origin and determine that they are better off in their new society. Minority group categories depicted by the cultural ecologists do not allow for the nuance and fluidity of within-group dynamics.[16] This study highlights the processes within schools that forge distinct interpretations and reactions toward schooling. It shows how the social and academic identity of Vietnamese students was shaped through their schooling experiences. The Dedicators stressed a competitive educational attainment, for instance, and the Team Players emphasized collaborative learning.

The institutional mechanisms and cultural processes proved powerful practices forging distinct social and academic experiences for Asian youth.[17] Students had different interpretations of the model minority image and their subsequent responses to these perceptions varied as well. Perceptions diverged depending on the academic community in which they were involved. Students clearly used the model minority profile to their advantage by acknowledging their teachers' and counselors' positive images of them and by forming strong peer networks to accomplish their academic goals. This pattern was consistently found for the Vietnamese students in both AP classes and the Medical Academy. The Medical Academy Vietnamese students, however, looked more critically at the Asian model stereotype and were quick to point out inconsistencies.

Research, policy, and practice must take notice of the harmful effects of race and ethnic stereotypes. The model minority stereotype lumps all Asians into one category, ignoring within-group differences. This chapter exposes differences even within high achieving Vietnamese high school students.

Within the school context, different types of academic structures and cultures forge different forms of student agency. In this study, Asian students navigated between their perceptions of themselves and what others thought of them. The institutional mechanisms and cultural phenomena mediate the process of identity formation and subsequent perceptions and reactions to schooling. The positive impacts of community solidarity and networking, along with exposure to those of different cultures, suggest models of success for students of all backgrounds.

Notes

1. Barringer, H. R., Takeuchi, D. T., & Xenos, P. (1990). Education, occupational prestige, and income of Asian Americans. *Sociology of Education, 63,* 27–43; Chun, K.-T. (1995). The myth of Asian American success and its educational ramifications. In D. T. Nakanishi & T. Y. Nishida (Eds.), *The Asian American educational experience: A source book for teachers and students.* New York: Routledge; Hu, A. (1989). Asian Americans: Model minority or double minority? *Amerasia Journal, 15,* 243–257; Lee, S. J. (1996). *Unraveling the "model minority" stereotype: Listening to Asian American youth.* New York: Teachers College Press; Lee, S. J. (2001). More than "model minorities" or "delinquents": A look at Hmong American high school students. *Harvard Educational Review, 71*(3), 505–528; Wong, M. G. (1980, October). Model students? Teachers' perceptions and expectations of their Asian and white students. *Sociology of Education, 53,* 236–246.

2. Barringer, Takeuchi, & Xenos (1990); Lee (1996, 2001); Portes, A., & MacLeod, D. (1996). Educational progress of children of immigrants: The roles of class, ethnicity, and school context. *Sociology of Education, 69,* 255–275; Sue, S., & Okazaki, S. (1990). Asian-American educational achievements: A phenomenon in search of an explanation. *American Psychologist, 45*(8), 913–920.

3. Caplan, N., Choy, M. H., & Whitmore, J. K. (1991). *Children of the boat people: A study of educational success.* Ann Arbor: University of Michigan Press; Mordkowitz, E. R., & Ginsberg, H. P. (1987). Early academic socialization of successful Asian-American college students. *Quarterly Newsletter of the Laboratory of Comparative Human Cognition, 9,* 85–91; Kitano, E.-Y. (1969). *Japanese Americans: The evolution of a subculture.* Englewood Cliffs, NJ: Prentice Hall.

4. Lee (1996).

5. Hirschman, C., & Wong, M. G. (1986, September). The extraordinary achievement of Asian Americans: A search for historical evidence and explanations. *Social Forces, 65*(1), 1–27; Okutsu, J. K. (1989). Pedagogic "hegemonicide" and the Asian American student. *Amerasia, 15*(1), 233–242; Sue & Okazaki (1990).

6. Okutsu (1989).

7. Sue & Okazaki (1990).

8. Matute-Bianchi, M. E. (1986). Ethnic identities and patterns of school success and failure among Mexican-descent and Japanese-American students in a California high school: An ethnographic analysis. *American Journal of Education, 95*(1), 233–255; Ogbu, J. U. (1987). Variability in minority school performance: A problem in search of an explanation. *Anthropology and Education Quarterly, 18*(4), 312–334; Ogbu, J. U., & Matute-Bianchi, M. E. (1986). Understanding sociocultural factors: Knowledge, identity, and school adjustment. In California State Department of Education (Ed.), *Beyond language: Social and cultural factors in schooling language minority students* (pp. 73–142). Los Angeles: California State Department of Education, Evaluation, Dissemination, and Assessment Center.

9. Conchas, G. Q. (2001). Structuring failure and success: Understanding the variability in Latino school engagement. *Harvard Educational Review, 71*(3), 475–504; Conchas, G. Q., & Goyette, K. A. (2002). Family and non-family roots of social capital among Vietnamese and Mexican American children. *Research in Sociology of Education, 13*, 41–72; Lee (1996, 2001).

10. Gibson, M. A. (1988). *Accommodation without assimilation: Sikh immigrants in an American high school.* Ithaca, NY: Cornell University Press.

11. Bankston, C. L., and Zhou, M. (1995). Effects of minority-language literacy on the academic achievement of Vietnamese youth in New Orleans. *Sociology of Education, 68*, 1–17; Portes and MacLeod (1996).

12. Conchas (2001); Mehan, H., Villanueva, I., Hubbard, L., & Lintz, A. (1996). *Constructing school success: The consequences of untracking low-achieving students.* Cambridge, MA: Cambridge University Press.

13. Bankston and Zhou (1995).

14. Suárez-Orozco (1989).

15. Ogbu, U. (1991). Involuntary minorities. In M. A. Gibson and J. U. Ogbu (Eds.), *Minority status and schooling* (pp. 3–22). New York: Garland.

16. Lee (1996, 2001).

17. Conchas (2001); Mehan, Villanueva, Hubbard, & Lintz (1996).

GILBERTO Q. CONCHAS *is assistant professor in administration, planning, and social policy at the Graduate School of Education at Harvard University.*

CRISTINA C. PÉREZ *is a graduate student in the College of Ethnic Studies at San Francisco State University.*

This chapter seeks to unpack ethnicity through a close examination of ethnic language schools and the ethnic system of supplementary education in the immigrant Chinese community in the United States. It sheds light on the specific ways in which ethnic community organizations contribute to educational achievement.

4

Ethnic language schools and the development of supplementary education in the immigrant Chinese community in the United States

Min Zhou, Xi-Yuan Li

PAST AND RECENT studies have consistently found that ethnicity has varied effects on the educational achievement of immigrant children. These studies show that, even after controlling for parental socioeconomic characteristics and family incomes, Asians outperform non-Hispanic whites who, in turn, outperform blacks and Hispanics by a significantly large margin. Much of the intellectual debate on intergroup differences in academic outcomes centers around two concepts—*culture* (emphasizing the role of internal agency along with group-specific values, norms, and behavioral patterns as well as the extent to which ethnic cultures fit the requirements of the mainstream society) and *structure* (emphasizing the

NEW DIRECTIONS FOR YOUTH DEVELOPMENT, NO. 100, WINTER 2003 © WILEY PERIODICALS, INC.

role of societal stratification and the opportunities and constraints that the system of stratification creates, moving some groups ahead in society while holding back others).

Just how culture and structure interact to affect intergenerational mobility is the crux of the matter. In this chapter, we seek to unpack ethnicity through a close examination of ethnic language schools and the ethnic system of supplementary education in the immigrant Chinese community in the United States. In doing so, we first briefly discuss the theoretical framing of the role of the ethnic community in shaping immigrant children's development. We then trace the developments of Chinese language schools and other child- or youth-centered ethnic institutions to illustrate how ethnicity can affect an advantageous environment yielding positive academic outcomes. We focus on exploring how ethnic institutions function not only to promote the value of education but also to ensure its actualization. We argue that ethnicity cannot be simplified into either a structural or a cultural measure, but rather it encompasses values and behavioral patterns that are constantly interacting with both internal and external structural circumstances.

Unpacking ethnicity: Community forces, social capital, and the ethnic environment

Existing literature has long recognized the role of the ethnic community in immigrant settlement and adaptation. According to classical assimilation theories, new immigrants, with little English language proficiency, few marketable or transferable skills, and limited information about their new homeland, cluster in ethnic enclaves upon arrival and rely on coethnic networks and social institutions to find housing, jobs, and their way around. But they are expected to eventually move out of the enclave as they achieve socioeconomic mobility. Ethnic institutions are initially instrumental in reorganizing immigrants' economic and social lives and in alleviating social problems arising from migration and ghetto living. In the long run, however, these institutions either dissolve, fading into merely symbolic significance as no newer groups support them, or act as roadblocks inhibiting assimilation.

In reality, however, the mechanisms by which ethnic communities influence the social mobility of group members and their children are complex and subtle. Because different immigrant groups vary in their initial modes of entry and subsequent societal reception, they vary in their orientation toward their host society, in their coping strategies, and in their abilities to muster and mobilize resources to shape an advantageous ethnic community.[1] Hence, the constituents of ethnic diversity in America are unequal; for some, maintaining a distinctive attachment to an ethnic community can facilitate intergenerational mobility of ethnic group members while for others it inhibits mobility. Native-born African American parents, Latino immigrant parents, or Asian immigrant parents all stress the value of education, and the children of these racial groups all agree that education is imperative in occupational achievement. Yet only Asian Americans as a group seem to have an upper hand in actualizing that value. In our view, what determines a child's development is not merely parental racial backgrounds and socioeconomic characteristics but also the immediate social environment in which the child grows up. For racial minority groups this social environment is often ethnically specific, manifested in observable neighborhood-based ethnic institutions and in interpersonal relations among those who interact in those institutions.

We frame our study of Chinese language schools and the ethnic system of supplementary education in terms of how these schools create an ethnic environment conducive to immigrant children's educational achievement. Two theoretical conceptions are of vital relevance: community forces and social capital. Ogbu conceptualizes community forces as specific beliefs, interpretations, and coping strategies that an ethnic group adopts in response to its societal treatment. Some racial minority groups manage to turn their distinctive cultural heritage into a kind of ethnic armor and establish a sense of collective dignity that enables them to cope psychologically, even in the face of exclusion and discrimination, by keeping the host society at arm's length. Others, however, internalize socially imposed inferiority as part of their collective self-definition. This in turn fosters an "oppositional outlook" toward the dominant group and mainstream institutions, including education.[2] In this case, symbolic expressions of ethnicity and ethnic empowerment may hinder rather than facilitate social mobility.

Community forces shape a particular ethnic environment while also mediating the process of social capital formation in that environment. Coleman defines social capital as a closed system of social networks inherent within a community that promotes cooperative behavior and serves specific needs of its members.[3] Despite heated debates on how social capital should be precisely defined and measured, it is generally agreed that social capital is lodged not in the individual but in the structure of social organizations, in patterns of social relations, or in processes of interactions between individuals and organizations. Portes suggests, "social capital stands for the ability of actors to secure benefits by virtue of memberships in social networks or other social structures."[4] Community forces dictate the orientation, coping strategies, and corresponding behaviors of different ethnic groups in regard to mobility goals and means of achieving those goals. The ethnic community and its institutions provide crucial sites for coethnic members to rebuild social relations and networks that may have been disrupted through migration. One way to understand how a particular ethnic environment is affected by community forces and social capital is to examine the density and variety of ethnic institutions in a given ethnic community and the extent to which these institutions are oriented toward social mobility.[5]

Development of Chinese language schools and ethnic systems of supplementary education

Chinese language schools date back to the late 1880s in the United States.[6] Just like other ethnic language schools in the immigrant German, Scandinavian, Jewish, and Japanese communities, Chinese language schools aimed to preserve language and cultural heritage in the second and succeeding generations. However, unlike other ethnic language schools, early Chinese language schools did not function to facilitate assimilation because of the enactment of the Chinese Exclusion Act of 1882 and the resulting discriminatory practices against the Chinese.

Prior to World War II there were few women, families, and children living in Chinatowns. These bachelors' societies had gender ratios of nearly twenty-seven men to one woman in 1890, nine to one in 1910, gradually approximating parity in 1940 with two men for every one woman. The shortage of women combined with the "paper son" phenomenon and other illegal entry of young men stifled the formation of "normal" families and the natural reproduction of the ethnic population. But a small second generation became increasingly visible among the aging bachelors after the 1930s. Like other racial minority children, however, the children of Chinese immigrants were not permitted to attend public schools with white children. As they reached adulthood, few were able to find jobs in the mainstream economy that were commensurate with their levels of education.

It was against this historical backdrop that Chinese language schools emerged and developed, first appearing in San Francisco's Chinatown in 1884. Early Chinese language schools were mostly private, financed primarily by tuition and donations from churches, temples, family associations, and Chinese businesses. There were also "public" Chinese language schools financed by the Chinese government. Each school was governed by a board consisting of mostly elite members from ethnic organizations and businesses in Chinatown. Schools typically had one or two part-time teachers, instruction was in Cantonese, and classes were held daily for three to four hours in the evenings and on Saturday mornings, usually in the basement of a teacher's home or in a room inside a family association building. Chinatown's children attended segregated public schools during regular school hours on weekdays and spent many more hours after school, on weekends, and during summer vacations learning Chinese in ethnic language schools.

Wherever there was a sizable Chinese enclave there was at least one Chinese language school. Chinese language schools were embedded in the organizational structure of the immigrant community and were the only ethnic institutions serving children. Like other ethnic organizations in Chinatown, earlier Chinese language schools had very little contact with mainstream institutions: the primary aim was to provide the children with a basic education and with cultural and language proficiency. Children attended Chinese language schools in their neighborhoods after regular school as a matter of course, with little questioning. Parents believed that proficiency in the Chinese language was practical for their children because their children's future options were limited to either returning to China or finding jobs in Chinatowns. Parents also believed that a strong Chinese identity and ethnic pride instilled in the children through Chinese cultural and moral teachings were necessary to help the children cope with racism and discrimination. Though most children lacked enthusiasm and interest, many recognized the practical value of Chinese schooling because their future prospects were largely limited to Chinatowns or China.

The repeal of the Chinese Exclusion Act in 1943 marked a new era for Chinese American community development. For the first time in history, immigrant Chinese and their offspring were legally allowed and encouraged to participate in American society and the ethnic community began to reorient itself from sojourning to putting down roots and reinforcing its commitment to socioeconomic integration. Meanwhile, the coming of age of a visibly large second generation resulting from several decades of Chinese exclusion quietly altered the demographic makeup of the bachelor's society, turning it more and more into a family-centered community. By 1960, the sex ratio had become more balanced and the U.S. born outnumbered the foreign born. Contemporary Chinese immigration, which had accelerated since the late 1970s, brought further demographic changes. By 2000, the Chinese American population had grown to a total of 2,879,636 persons; 58 percent were foreign born, and more than half lived in the suburbs.

The openness in mainstream American society does not automatically guarantee desirable outcomes of economic mobility and social integration. Decades of legal exclusion, social isolation, discrimination, and persistent racial stereotyping have left the Chinese with one practically feasible route for upward mobility—public education. Whereas children's education was never an issue for survival in a society full of bachelors and sojourners, it has now become an urgent and central issue for immigrant families and the entire ethnic group. Hence, the development of Chinese language schools has undergone cycles of decline, revival, and rapid growth.

Between World War II and the 1960s, Chinese language schools experienced a period of decline due to pressures to assimilate. Immigrant children started to question the necessity of Chinese schooling and the practical value of Chinese language proficiency. Public schools reinforced their wishes by encouraging them to break away from ethnic language schools. The rationale of public educators was that ethnic education would impede students' social and intellectual developments and place too much burden on young minds. Other factors that caused Chinese language schools to decline included the aging of the teachers, who were mostly non-English speaking and slow to adjust to changes; the rigidity of the curriculum and teaching methods; residential dispersion; and the opening of various educational and vocational opportunities outside Chinatown. Thus, going to Chinese school became a burden on the child and a source of parent-child conflict. Nevertheless, under parental pressure, many children continued to attend Chinese language schools, though most dropped out by the sixth grade. Many parents were ambivalent as well; while many wanted their children to learn English and excel in school, they feared that they would lose their children if their children became too Americanized.

Characteristics of contemporary Chinese language schools

Since the 1970s there has been a revival and rapid growth of ethnic businesses and institutions in Chinatowns and suburban Chinese communities (referred to as Chinese ethnoburbs.)[7] Chinese language schools and a wide variety of child- and youth-centered ethnic institutions are among the most noticeable development, constituting a comprehensive system of supplementary education.

The National Council of Associations of Chinese Language Schools in 1994 counted a total of 643 registered Chinese language schools in the United States serving 82,675 K–12 students.[8]

Traditional Chinese language schools located in Chinatowns have been under pressure to change. Today the New York Chinese Schools run by the Chinatown Consolidated Benevolent Association, once the quasi-government of Chinatown, are perhaps the largest child- and youth-oriented organizations in inner-city Chinatowns. These schools enroll about four thousand children annually, from preschool to twelfth grade, in their 137 Chinese language classes and more than 10 specialty classes (such as band, choir, piano, cello, violin, T'ai chi, ikebana, dancing, and Chinese painting). These classes run from 3:00 to 6:30 P.M. daily after regular school hours. Students usually spend one hour on regular school homework and two hours on Chinese language or other selected specialties. The school also has English classes for immigrant youths and adult immigrant workers.[9]

New Chinese language schools also sprung up in both Chinatowns and Chinese ethnoburbs, started by educated Taiwanese immigrants and then by international students and well-educated professional immigrants from mainland China. The majority of suburban Chinese schools affiliated with the Southern California United Chinese School Association were initially established by Taiwanese immigrants in the mid- or late 1970s. In the early 1990s, the Hua Xia Chinese School was established as a Saturday school in a New Jersey suburb by immigrant Chinese from the mainland. It has now expanded into fourteen branch campuses in suburbs along the northeastern seaboard from Connecticut to Pennsylvania, serving more than five thousand students and shifting its admission to "everyone, regardless of his or her gender, race, color of skin, religion, nationality and blood ties."[10] Similarly, the Hope Chinese School started as a small weekend Saturday school in a Washington, D.C., suburb for professional Chinese immigrant families from mainland China in the early 1990s and has now grown into five campuses in suburban towns in Maryland and Virginia, enrolling more than two thousand students. The community has also witnessed the development of various child- and youth-oriented private institutions, including after-school tutoring centers, college preparation institutes, and music-arts-sports programs, as well as daycare facilities and preschools. These private institutions range from transnational enterprises with headquarters or branches in Taiwan and mainland China to small-scale one-person or mom-and-pop operations. By offering various academic and cultural enrichment programs and after-school care, Chinese language schools and child- or youth-centered private institutions form a sophisticated system of supplementary education accessible mainly by Chinese immigrant families.

Today's Chinese language schools, both in and out of Chinatown, are distinctive compared to those established prior to World War II. Their primary goal is to assist immigrant families in their efforts to push their children to excel in American public schools, to get into prestigious colleges and universities, and to eventually attain well-paying, high-status professions that secure a decent living in the United States. These organizations reflect the traditional pragmatism of Chinese immigrant families, which is only U.S.-centered rather than China-centered, as articulated in the words of a Chinese immigrant, "I hope to accomplish nothing but three things [in the U.S.]: to own a home, to be my own boss, and to send my children to the Ivy League." Parents are enthusiastic about sending their children to Chinese language schools not because they think that Chinese is the only thing that is important. Rather, many parents are implicitly dissatisfied with American public schools and believe that Chinese language schools and other ethnic supplementary institutions are instrumental in ensuring that their children meet parental expectations.[11]

Unlike traditional Chinese language schools, which were relatively homogeneous and rigid in institutional form and governance, today's schools have become more diverse and flexible. They are either nonprofit (including church, temple, community, or family association sponsored schools) or for-profits (independent enterprises functioning in the same way as other ethnic businesses). Most schools in Chinatowns or Chinese ethnoburbs offer regular weekday (3 to 6 P.M. daily after school), weekend (Saturday or Sunday half-day), and summer programs (day schools or overseas camps), as well as programs during spring and Christmas breaks (day camps). Scheduling accommodates the needs of dual-worker families living in the ethnic community. Other suburban Chinese schools are mostly half-day Saturday or Sunday schools because families tend to disperse into noncoethnic neighborhoods as far apart as twenty to thirty miles.

Schools are mainly financed by student tuitions, but nonprofits are supported by donations and community fundraising as well. Nonprofits are free or charge nominal fees. Tuitions in for-profits vary depending on the type of program and enrollment, ranging from $70 to $250, and can be as high as $400 per semester for a typical weekday after-school program or a weekend school program, with extra fees for enrollment in special programs that are offered in the schools. Private lessons range from $10 to $50 per hour. Each school has a principal, a part-time staff, and teachers. It is governed by a board consisting of parents, teachers, ethnic business owners, and community leaders. Members of the governing board also tend to be parents themselves. Nonprofits rely heavily on parents who volunteer to act as teacher aides, chauffeurs to pick up or drop off students, fundraising workers, and even janitors. Such parental voluntarism is also evident in for-profits. Many Chinese schools have parent volunteer associations modeled after the parent-teacher associations in public schools. Parental involvement is direct and intense in Chinese schools, but similar involvement is minimal in U.S. public schools because of language and cultural barriers.

Unlike traditional schools where the teaching of Chinese language and culture was at the core of the curriculum, today's Chinese language schools have shifted to a more comprehensive, well-rounded curriculum that complements the requirements of public education by grade level and college preparation. Language teaching no longer takes priority in most of today's Chinese language schools, and Chinese classics have been almost completely removed from the curriculum. Teachers, staff members, and even parents habitually use a mixture of English and Chinese to communicate with the children. Schools now offer a variety of academic and tutoring programs in such subjects as English, social studies, math, and the sciences, as well as in college preparation (including SAT preparation) in addition to the Chinese language. They also offer extracurricular programs such as youth leadership training, public speaking, modern and folk dancing, chorus, music (piano, violin, drums, and Chinese stringed instruments), drama, Chinese painting, calligraphy, origami, martial arts, Chinese chess and Go, and sports (tennis, ping-pong ball, and basketball being the most popular). Some Chinese schools have excellent Chinese language programs (mostly in Mandarin) that aim to assist students in gaining high school foreign language credits and in excelling on the SAT II Chinese language test.

While Chinese language teaching is balanced with other academic enrichment, tutoring, and recreational programs, the focus on moral teaching and the passing on of cultural heritage is more subtle in today's Chinese schools. When schools are in session, these institutions provide a cultural environment where the children are surrounded by other Chinese and pressured to act (and thus feel) Chinese. Teachers reinforce the values of filial piety, respect for authority, hard work, and discipline. Also, during traditional Chinese holiday seasons, such as the Chinese New Year, the Dragon Festival in the spring, and the Mid-Autumn Moon Festival, Chinese schools participate in celebratory parades, evening shows, and other community events such as sports and choral or dance festivals. Participation in these cultural activities not only exposes children to their cultural heritage, reaffirming their ethnic identity, but also provides opportunities for the children to work closely with their parents and other adults in the community on common projects.

Spillover effects

In essence, Chinese language schools and the ethnic system of supplementary education are designed "by the parents, for the parents," as one school's motto says. More often than not, immigrant Chinese parents measure success not merely by their own occupational achievements but by their children's educational achievements. If a child goes to an Ivy League college, his or her parents feel rewarded and are admired and respected as successful parents. If their children are less successful, they lose face. In this respect, Chinese schools and the relevant ethnic institutions emerge to respond directly to parents' desires for success. On the one hand, they produce a community force driving children to attain educational success on their parents' terms. Flashy names such as "Little Harvard," "Ivy League School," "Little Ph.D. Early Learning Center" (a preschool), "Stanford-to-Be Prep School," "IQ180," and "Hope Buxiban (Tutoring)" are illustrative. Advertisements in the Chinese language newspapers are full of such promises as to "bring out the best in your child," "turn your child into a well-rounded superstar," "escort your child into your dream school," and "opening the door to UC admission," which are carefully crafted to attract parents' attention. On the other hand, these ethnic institutions also provide child care and after-school care for working families. While some of these schools may not have many structured programs, existing simply to keep children under adult supervision, most offer a variety of programs and activities at flexible after-school hours along with drop-off and pick-up services.

The effects extend far beyond after-school services, however. For parents, Chinese language schools provide an important physical site where formerly unrelated immigrants come to socialize and rebuild social ties. Reconnecting with coethnics often helps ease psychological and social isolation. The coethnic ties that are rebuilt may not be as strong as the ones that existed in traditional Chinatowns of the past. Nonetheless, they serve as a bridge that connects immigrants to, rather than isolates them from, the mainstream society by making their social life richer and more comfortable. One Chinese parent likened the suburban Chinese school to a church:

We are nonreligious and don't go to church. So coming to Chinese school weekly is like going to church for us. While our children are in class, we parents don't just go home, because we live quite far away. We hang out here and participate in a variety of things that we organize for ourselves, including dancing, fitness exercise, seminars on the stock market, family financial management, and children's college prep. I kind of look forward to going to the Chinese school on Saturdays because that is the only time we can socialize with our own people in our native language. I know some of our older kids don't like it that much. When they complain, I simply tell them, "This is not a matter of choice, you must go."[12]

Chinese language schools also serve as an intermediate ground between the immigrant home and the American school. They help immigrant parents (especially those who do not speak English well) to learn about the American educational system. It facilitates their making the best of the system in serving their children without requiring involvement in formal schools and their parent-teacher associations. Through these ethnic institutions, immigrant parents are indirectly but effectively connected to formal schools and are well-informed of the specifics crucial for their children's educational success. The social capital arising from participating in Chinese schools and other ethnic institutions is extremely valuable in serving this particular goal.

Chinese language schools foster a sense of civic duty in immigrants, who are often criticized for their lack of civic participation. In ethnic institutions, many parents volunteer their time and energy to various tasks ranging from decision making, fundraising, and serving as teaching assistants, event organizers, chauffeurs, security guards, and janitors. Parents also take the initiative in organizing community events such as Chinese and American holiday celebrations.

The spillover effects on children are equally significant. First, Chinese language schools and other relevant ethnic institutions offer an alternative space where children can express and share their feelings about growing up in immigrant Chinese families. A Chinese schoolteacher says:

It is very important to allow youths to express themselves in their own terms without any parental pressure. Chinese parents usually have very high expectations of their children. When children find it difficult to meet these expectations and do not have an outlet for their frustration and anxiety, they tend to become alienated and lost on the streets. But when they are around others who have similar experiences, they are more likely to let out their feelings and come to terms with their current situation.

Moreover, these ethnic institutions provide unique opportunities for immigrant children to form a different set of peer group networks, giving them more leverage in negotiating parent-child relations at home. In immigrant Chinese families, parents are usually less restrictive when their children socialize with Chinese rather than American friends. Because they may know the parents of their children's Chinese friends or because they feel they can communicate with the Chinese parents if things go wrong, they are more comfortable with these arrangements. When youth elicit their parents' anxiety and objection, they may use their Chinese friendship network as an effective bargaining chip to avoid conflict. In the case of interracial dating, for example, a Chinese girl may tell her mother that she is studying with a friend from Chinese school while running off with her non-Chinese boyfriend, avoiding an intense confrontation with her mother.

These ethnic institutions also function to nurture ethnic identity and pride among Chinese youth who may otherwise reject the Chinese identity due to pressures to assimilate. In Chinese schools they are exposed to something quite different from what they learn in their formal schools. For example, they recite classical Chinese poems and Confucian sayings about family values, behavioral and moral guidelines, and the importance of schooling. They listen to Chinese fables and legends and learn to sing Chinese folk songs, which reveal various aspects of Chinese history and culture. Such cultural exposure reinforces family values and heightens a sense of "Chineseness," helping children to relate to the Chinese culture without feeling embarrassed. A Chinese school principal clarified that "these kids are here because their parents sent them. They are usually not very motivated in learning Chinese *per se*, and we do not push them too hard. Language teaching is only part of our mission. An essential part of our mission is to enlighten these kids about their own cultural heritage, so that they show respect for their parents and feel proud of being Chinese."

More important, being in this particular ethnic environment helps alleviate the bicultural conflicts that run rampant in many immigrant families. As Betty Lee Sung observed in her study of immigrant children in New York City's Chinatown, bicultural conflicts are "moderated to a large degree because there are other Chinese children around to mitigate the dilemmas that they encounter. When they are among their own, the Chinese ways are better known and better accepted. The Chinese customs and traditions are not denigrated to the degree that they would be if the immigrant child were the only one to face the conflict on his or her own."[13]

The ethnic effect is by no means uniformly positive. Tremendous pressures on the children as well as on the parents to achieve can lead to intense intergenerational conflict, rebellious behavior, alienation from the networks that are supposed to assist them, and even withdrawal from formal schools. A resourceful ethnic environment, however, by exerting similar pressures, can reinforce parental expectations. Children are motivated to learn and do well in school because they believe that education is the only way to escape their parents' control. This motivation, while arising from parental pressure and being reinforced through participation in the ethnic institutions, often leads to desirable outcomes. A nonprofit program organizer summed it up in these words: "Well, tremendous pressures create problems for sure. However, you've got to realize that we are not living in an ideal environment. Without these pressures you would probably see as much adolescent rebellion in the family, but a much *larger* proportion of kids failing. Our goal is to get these kids out into college, and for that we have been very successful."

Conclusion

Together with other ethnic institutions specializing in academic and extracurricular programs for children, today's Chinese language schools have grown into an ethnic system of supplementary education that is complementary to rather than competitive with formal education. Despite diversity in form, governance, and curriculum, today's Chinese language schools, nonprofit and for-profit alike, compete intensely with one another in offering services to immigrant families that are directly relevant to children's formal public education. Our study illustrates how ethnic institutions support the value of education and highlights the important effect of the immediate social environment between a child's home and formal school. As a Chinese school teacher remarked, "when you think of how much time these Chinese kids put in their studies after regular school, you won't be surprised why they succeed at such a high rate." It is this ethnic environment with enormous tangible and intangible benefits to the immigrant family that helps promote and actualize the value of education.

It should be noted, however, that the ethnic resources and social capital can be effective only to a certain point. While the social capital ensures that immigrant children will graduate from high school and get into college, beyond high school it may become constraining. Many children of Chinese immigrants, for example, limit their vocational trajectories, tending to concentrate in science and engineering. They may do so not only because their families pressure them to do so but also because their coethnic friends are taking the same paths. Unfortunately, after graduating from college they often lack the type of social networks that would facilitate their job placement and occupational mobility. In this respect, there is much room for improvement in the existing ethnic system of supplementary education.

Notes

1. Ogbu, J. U., & Simon, H. N. (1998). Voluntary and involuntary minorities. *Anthropology and Educational Quarterly, 29,* 2.

2. Ogbu, J. U. (1974). *The next generation: An ethnography of education in an urban neighborhood.* New York: Academic Press.

3. Coleman, J. S. (1990). *Foundations of social theory.* Cambridge, MA: Harvard University Press.

4. Portes, A. (1998). Social capital: Its origins and application in modern sociology. *Annual Review of Sociology, 24,* 4.

5. This case study is exploratory. The material presented in this section draws primarily on observations conducted by the authors at community events; in private homes, Chinese schools and other private educational institutions, religious and community-based organizations, and ethnic businesses; and on main business streets in New York's Chinatown between September and October 1994, in Los Angeles' Chinatown between July 1999 and December 2001, at a suburban Chinese school in Washington D.C. between Novem-

ber 2000 and May 2001, and in Los Angeles's Monterey Park between July 1999 and April 2003. Random interviews were conducted face-to-face on site or by phone. Both Chinese and English were used in face-to-face and telephone interviews. All names are pseudonyms to ensure anonymity.

6. Some noted that Chinese language schools dated as far back as the late 1840s, when Chinese laborers started to arrive in the United States in large numbers. See Fong, J. C. (2003). *Complementary education and culture in the global/local Chinese community*. San Francisco: China Books and Periodicals; Lai, H. M. (2000). Retention of the Chinese heritage: Language schools in America before World War II. In Chinese Historical Society of America (Ed.), *Chinese America: History and perspectives*, 2000. San Francisco: Chinese Historical Society of America; Wang, X. (1996). *A view from within: A case study of Chinese heritage community language schools in the United States*. Baltimore, MD: National Foreign Language Center, Johns Hopkins University.

7. *Ethnoburb* is a term developed by Wei Li to refer to suburban ethnic clustering of diverse groups in which no single racial ethnic group dominates. Los Angeles's Monterey Park is a typical ethnoburb. Li, W. (1997). Spatial transformation of an urban ethnic community from Chinatown to Chinese ethnoburb in Los Angeles. Unpublished doctoral dissertation, Department of Geography, University of Southern California.

8. Wang (1996); also cited and tabulated by states in Fong (2003).

9. Zhou, M. (1997). Social capital in Chinatown: The role of community-based organizations and families in the adaptation of the younger generation. In L. Weis & M. S. Seller (Eds.), *Beyond black and white: New voices, new faces in the United States schools*. Albany: State University of New York Press.

10. The by-law of Huaxia Chinese School. Retrieved March 2003 from http://www.hxcs.org/headquarters/organization/by-law.htm

11. Fong (2003).

12. Interview at the Hope Chinese School in Rockville, MD, December 2001.

13. Sung, B. L. (1987). *The adjustment experience of Chinese immigrant children in New York City*. Staten Island, NY: Center for Migration Studies, p. 126.

MIN ZHOU *is professor of sociology at the University of California, Los Angeles.*

XI-YUAN LI *is a visiting scholar at the University of California, Los Angeles.*

Using emergent theme analysis of qualitative inter-
view data in combination with quantitative survey
data, the role of religion in the lives of immigrant
youth was explored. Latino, Haitian, and Chinese
teenagers described, in their own rich words, the
significance of religion to them; their responses are
reflected in themes that point to the potential pro-
tective role of religion for some immigrant groups.

5

"He is everything": Religion's role in the lives of immigrant youth

Nora E. Thompson, Andrea G. Gurney

AS I APPROACHED the dimly lit, run-down building in one of Boston's large housing projects, the pervasive sense of hopelessness was unfortunately familiar. As I rounded the corner to the third floor landing, something felt different—it seemed brighter, less ominous. This landing wasn't empty. Pictures of saints and hand-written Bible verses were taped to the wall. Bumper stickers with the phrase *"Dios te amo"* ("God loves you") decorated the hallway. A postcard of the Virgin Mary in a frame much too big for the card hung over the front door. Someone had transformed this place into an inspirational oasis; it was an image that stayed with me.

NEW DIRECTIONS FOR YOUTH DEVELOPMENT, NO. 100, WINTER 2003 © WILEY PERIODICALS, INC.

Risk, resilience, and religion

Resilience is frequently conceptualized as an individual's positive response to stress and adversity.[1] Although there is variability in the definition of resilience, the underlying implication is that it reflects characteristics of the environment and the competent way in which an individual responds. Resilience rests on the dynamic integration of risk factors and protective resources (individual personality traits and environmental factors) in response to challenges.

Previous research has linked religiosity with resilience. Research studies indicate that religiosity promotes healthy family functioning. There is a growing body of research pertaining to the relationship between religiosity's effect on physical health, mental health, marital relationships, and parent-child interactions.[2] Religiosity is positively linked with social support and prosocial attitudes and has been associated with a warm parenting style in certain communities.[3] Religion, in all of these ways, is linked to the concept of resilience.

Immigration: A potential risk

The process of immigration is understood to be a stressor for youth. "Even under the best of circumstances, moving to a foreign country to begin a new life is stressful. . . . Adjusting to new living situations, different food, learning a new language, learning how to get around, making new friends, and all the other details of daily life in a new country create stress for both parents and children."[4] The stressors associated with immigration that have been considered in the research literature include social isolation, family disruption, unfamiliar school systems, racism, and urban poverty.[5] Although the process is stressful, immigrant youth do not have uniform responses to the experience. Some seem to thrive despite the many stressors; others experience negative consequences.[6] This variability of response, termed *multifinality*, suggests that an array of vulnerability and protective factors interact to create divergent developmental trajectories for immigrant youth.[7]

The risk and resiliency framework is particularly useful for the study of immigration in that it allows us to consider simultaneously both the stressors and the protective factors of a situation. This framework promotes consideration of the complex array of vulnerability and protective factors that are a part of an individual's developmental history. Rather than focusing on one aspect of or event in a person's development as a predictor of outcome, it is recommended that a person's entire life (including the multiple stressors and protective factors) be considered as all of the aspects and events interplay to predict future adjustment.

In studying resilient and nonresilient immigrant youth, it is important to consider what factors may be protective. A wide range of variables—broadly categorized as individual, family, and community-based—have been hypothesized to foster resilience. More specifically, there is growing evidence that religious belief, or faith, and the practice of religious ritual might be buffers from negative life events at the individual, familial, and community levels.[8]

Religion: A potential protector

There are various estimates regarding the percentage of the general population that identifies itself as religious. According to the 2000 U.S. Census, 91 percent of the population claims to be religious and 70 percent of the U.S. population are reportedly church or synagogue members. In one of the largest national surveys given to assess religious affiliation in the United States (a Gallup survey), approximately 92 percent of the respondents identified themselves as religious.[9] A Pew Research Center poll taken in 2001 reports that six in ten (61 percent) currently say religion plays a *very important* role in their lives. Additionally, religion is increasing in prominence in the United States. In the same poll, nearly eight in ten Americans say that religion's influence is growing; these 78 percent who see religion as gaining influence in American life surpass measures from years past.[10]

Research has indicated that religion, as it is personally and socially constructed, is protective in specific ways.[11] Religious adults, for example, report more adaptive strategies for dealing with life stresses and more optimistic and focused coping efforts, enhanced feeling of personal efficacy, and a stronger sense of community and social support than nonreligious adults.[12] Additionally, religion has been demonstrated to be important in the lives of urban youth.[13] Previous studies reveal that teenagers who attend church and are involved in a religious organization are less stressed, feel more supported, are more likely to abstain from sexual activity, and report more positive relationships with their parents. In many ethnic minority neighborhoods, the church is often viewed as central to the community.[14] Supports from church centers are both emotional and tangible.

Religion has also been demonstrated to be particularly significant in immigrant communities:

Religious institutions have always helped immigrants integrate into the countries that receive them and enabled them to stay connected to the countries they came from. . . . Religious institutions are extending and expanding their global operations such that migrants can remain active in sending-country religious groups and in the congregation that receives them. Religious participation incorporates migrants into strong transnational institutional networks where they acquire social citizenship and can seek protection, make claims, and articulate their interests, regardless of their political status. It integrates them into a transnational religious civil society that can complement or substitute for partial political membership.[15]

Within immigrant communities, religion has been highlighted as a key aspect of several immigrant cultures. Harker has shown some preliminary information that immigrant teenagers report religious belief and affiliation among the protective forces in their lives.[16] Bankston and Zhou have demonstrated that religious affiliation is protective for Vietnamese immigrant youth, particularly as it strengthens ethnic identification.[17] Within specific cultural groups of immigrants, religion has also begun to be understood as

critical. For Chinese immigrants, religious practice is both important and diverse. "There are over forty-five different ethnic groups
that reside in China. These groups practice various religions
including Buddhism, Taoism, Catholicism and other forms of
Christianity, and Islam. . . . Most Chinese believe in Confucianism,
which has a great deal of influence in China as well as in other parts
of Asia . . . [and] provides fundamental principles that guide behavior."[18] "The Haitian community represents a group tied together
by their religious beliefs—both Catholic and traditional practices—
as well as social clubs. A Haitian apostolate in Brooklyn has been
established with specific parishes, Haitian priests, liturgists, Bible
class in Creole, along with Creole hymnbooks."[19] Argueta-Bernal
describes the way religion is important in the Hispanic immigrant
community, how it is an important support for a people who con-
front the stress of immigration and minority status: "reliance and
belief on prayer, and the invocation of saints or spirits among Hispanics, produces a sense of security and well-being. It seems that
these belief systems and practices constitute a means of reducing
stress and tension for the Hispanic community."[20]

Given the overwhelming belief that religion has become increasingly important in the United States, in urban areas, and for immigrant communities, and given the potential protective role that
religion plays, there is surprisingly limited evidence regarding religion's place in the personal lives of immigrant youth. This chapter,
therefore, examines the ways religion is perceived in the lives of
immigrant youth. Using rich data, in the form of quotes from
immigrant youth, we examine the meanings and experiences associated with religion in Latino, Haitian, and Chinese youths' lives.
Implications for future research, practice, and policy are delineated
and discussed as well.

Immigrant youth: Reflections on religion

Our study was embedded in the Harvard Immigration Project, a
five-year longitudinal, interdisciplinary study of 350 immigrant
youth. These youth, ages fourteen to nineteen, had immigrated

from China, Haiti, Central America, Mexico, and the Dominican Republic. (Please see Chapter One by Suárez-Orozco & Todorova in this volume for a more detailed description of the Harvard Immigration Project.)

During the fifth year of the study, participants were given the opportunity, during individually administered interviews, to talk about religion in their lives. They were asked the following questions (the first yes-or-no, the second open-ended):

• Is religion or a belief in God important for you?
• In what ways is religion or God part of your life?

This combination of forced-choice and open-ended questions allowed the youth to identify and then explain in their own words the part that religion plays in their lives. From their stories and descriptions, central themes emerged. Across cultures, immigrant youth described ways in which they perceived religion as helpful. Religion served as a protective force in their lives.

In response to the first question, a surprising percentage of the teenagers stated that religion or belief in God is important in their lives. As seen in Table 5.1, the total percentage of Haitian, Chinese, and Latino youth who stated that religion or belief in God was an important part of their life was 76 percent. This significant percentage certainly attests to the significance of religion for these youth who have recently immigrated to the United States. Considering each immigrant group individually also revealed important distinctions between the immigrant groups. Of the forty-seven Haitian teenagers, forty-four stated that religion was indeed important to them; a mere three responded that it was not. Similarly, 137 of the

Table 5.1. Is religion or a belief in God important to you?

	Haitian N = 47	Chinese N = 71	Latino N = 177	Total
Yes	94%	28%	77%	76%
No	6%	72%	23%	24%

177 Latino immigrant youth stated that a belief in God was significant in their lives. This pattern was very different with the Chinese
teenagers; only twenty of the seventy-one Chinese youth said that
religion was important to them. (See Table 5.1 for percentages.)

It is important to note that there were no significant differences
for gender in the response pattern to this question. Given that gender has repeatedly been demonstrated to be a mediating variable
with youth, and immigrant youth specifically, it was surprising to
find that the young men and women in this study affirmed and
denied the importance of religion in their lives in equal percentages. This was true for each of the three ethnic groups. Table 5.2
illustrates the percentage of males and females, across ethnicities,
who affirm a belief in God.

Qualitative responses

As we began to examine the responses from the participants to the
question "What role does religion play in your life?" we were
struck by how articulate and expressive the youth were. They were
able to describe in their own words the many ways that
religion is important to them. From this one question, asked of
all ethnic groups, common themes emerged. Whether it was a
fourteen-year-old Haitian immigrant or a nineteen-year-old
Latino immigrant, there were similarities in the ideas they
expressed; these similarities were grouped into overarching
themes, of which there were eight. Although the emergent themes
are helpful ways of organizing the generated responses, the real

**Table 5.2. Percentage of group affirming that
religion or a belief in God is important to them**

	Males	*Females*
Total	80%	75%
Haitian	95%	96%
Chinese	25%	30%
Latino	94%	94%

power of this study is in the words the immigrant youth used to describe a very personal phenomenon.

Profession of faith

"I believe in God" were the words spoken by a fifteen-year-old Central American girl. It was as simple as that in her mind. A Haitian boy stated, "I believe in God—He is my Savior"; and a Chinese girl said, "I place God first in everything I do." It was as if they were being asked a ridiculous question and could only reply with a straightforward, factual statement. "You have to believe that there is something that you can believe in—you need to have faith. I know how, but I don't know how to explain it," one fifteen-year-old Dominican girl stated. Participants frequently included a strong profession of their belief or faith as part of their response. As a seventeen-year-old Dominican girl asserted, "It's very important for me because my mother raised us to believe in God in the beginning. He is everything in my life. I believe, He is all my support." These teenagers talked about something real to them and yet difficult to describe. Whether it was a simple acknowledgement of the existence of God or an encompassing expression of faith, these responses reflected their unquestioning belief as they professed their faith.

Help

Not only did many youth talk about their undeniable faith, but they also spoke of their perception of a very real and tangible help that God or spiritual powers provided for them. "If I got a problem that I could not figure out, I would pray. I would talk to God and ask God for an answer," said a seventeen-year-old Chinese boy. "Any problem, you ask Him for help, and He helps you," said a fifteen-year-old Mexican girl. A fifteen-year-old Dominican girl put it simply: "God helps in difficult times." The help that these teenagers spoke about was experienced as very real and tangible. "Just the fact that God is looking after you. If you have problems, you know where to get help." God was a helper to them—a God who helped solve problems or hardships, and also a God whom they could turn to in prayer and thus feel supported. "The more we pray, the less accidents we'll have," said a fifteen-year-old Mexican boy.

Many spoke about God as a helper and friend, someone they could turn to when things were tough, and someone or something that provided hope. "When you have problems you can say 'Oh God, help me to withstand this,'" believes a seventeen-year-old Dominican boy. A Chinese boy said that religion or belief in God "will be important when one is hopeless. It gives you hope and a future." Similarly, a Haitian boy said, "He helps with who you are—without God we wouldn't be here. He helps you move on with things you find difficult." As evident from their words, these youth found hope and help in the God about whom they spoke.

For some teenage respondents, help was experienced in the form of protection. As one Haitian boy stated, "I believe in God, it helps me. It protects my life from bad things, like the devil." A fifteen-year-old Mexican boy said, "I am protected, kept away from evil." Thus, whether help is derived in the form of tangible aid, companionship, protection, or a greater sense of safety, or in the sense of changed outcomes, a perceived awareness of support from a higher being is significant in the lives of these immigrant youth. Their words are powerful; their stories are powerful as well. "This is the reason we were able to come live in the United States. God helps me so that everything will come out well, so that I could have made it from Santo Domingo to live here."

Ritual

Many of the immigrant youth, when asked how religion or belief in God is important to them, talked about a consistency and stability that derived from religious activities. "I love God. I will always love God. I always pray before I go to sleep and before I eat," a thirteen-year-old Central American girl stated. "I pray every night. It's important!" and "We burn the incense" were responses from Chinese girls that were indicative of a regular practice or participation in a ritual. Likewise, a Chinese boy stated, "My family would make offerings to the folk deities, during the

Chinese festivals." When a Haitian boy was asked in what ways religion or a belief in God was important to him he stated, "Worshiping him. Go to church, and pray for your family." These were merely a part of his routine—what he had learned and believed in doing. A fifteen-year-old Mexican girl spoke to this continuity, sense of stability, and internalization when she replied, "It's part of me—since I was a small girl, I went to Catholic school." This regular practice—this participation in a religious ritual or ceremony—certainly did appear to be a part of who these teenagers had become; for many it was an integral part.

Culture and family

Religion not only was an important part of the immigrant youths' identity and sense of self, but it also appeared to provide a strong connection to one's familial and cultural identity. A fourteen-year-old Mexican girl stated, "I grew up believing in God, same as my family. And with the idea that one has to go to church and be good. I grew up believing in religion. It is something my family has taught me." A Haitian girl said that religion "brings me closer to my Haitian people," and a Haitian boy asserted, "At First Haitian Baptist church, there are strong people who my family can trust and go to." Their religious belief is a part of their family, their culture, and "provides [them] with . . . a sense of belonging."

Behavioral control

Religion or a belief in God often provided immigrant youth with guidelines and ways in which they should live their lives. "When my friends ask me to do something, I would use the religious perspectives to analyze the things and then decide whether òr not to do it." For this fifteen-year-old Chinese girl, her belief system was a framework, a lens through which she made decisions. Similarly, another Chinese girl stated, "It helps me to decide what is right and wrong. When I am in trouble, I pray. It gives me a feeling of relief."

Many of the teenagers spoke about concrete ways in which their religious belief influenced and spoke into their lives, actions, and behaviors. "It teaches me to respect people and not to steal," one Haitian girl commented. A Chinese boy remarked that religion was important to him because "[I] stay away from bad stuff—like sex and drugs." Another stated that religion helps by "telling me things that I am not supposed to do, such as you shouldn't live with somebody if you are not married to him" (fifteen-year-old Dominican girl). Similarly, a fourteen-year-old Mexican girl commented that her religious belief speaks into her life about things like "How to keep my virginity until marriage, to marry in the church." These are specific ways in which these immigrant youth relied on and looked to their religious belief.

For some, a sense of fear and punishment was associated with their religious belief. The words of a fifteen-year-old Dominican girl captured this best: "I have faith and I believe that when you do something bad God will punish you." This notion of an omnipresent and all-powerful God exerts a powerful influence on her thoughts and behaviors. Similarly, a seventeen-year-old Central American boy stated, "One thinks about what can happen, and being religious, sometimes it stops you from doing something." Thus, for many of these immigrant youth, their religion or belief in God served as a moral compass for their lives—pointing to directions and answers, revealing a "right" and "wrong" way, and providing boundaries.

Existential meaning

Along with referring to their belief as an external compass, immigrant youth also spoke of an internal peace that accompanied their faith. Religion provided for them a meaning for their existence; their belief in God or spirituality gave them a sense that life has a particular purpose or meaning. This sense of communion with a higher being is expressed most poignantly in the words of a fifteen-year-old girl from Central America: "There is something up there that makes this world, you have to believe. Here is a reason—to make you treasure life. That's what made your life." She seemed to possess a keen awareness of a being beyond herself, one whom she believes in and has a relationship with, one who perhaps provides hope and meaning.

Sense of worth

Many of these youth also related their belief in God to a feeling of self-worth. A fourteen-year-old girl from Mexico stated, "It's important because in that way I can have faith in myself." It seemed as if because she knew that a God loved her and believed in her, she could then believe more in herself. A Haitian girl spoke about God forgiving her; perhaps this made it easier for her to forgive and care about herself. Along the same lines, a fifteen-year-old boy from Mexico said that religion or belief in God "helps us believe in ourselves, in that we can get ahead in life." In their own words, these immigrant youth were talking about self-worth, self-value, and a sense of personal efficacy.

Relationship

An overarching theme interwoven in many responses was a sense of a personal relationship with God. A seventeen-year-old girl from Central America talked about this explicitly when she stated, "It's very important. I can count on Him. He doesn't tell my secrets. He knows about me." She speaks of a friendship—someone who knows her, who knows her secrets and will keep them, someone she can turn to and count on being there. It sounds as if she is referring to a dear, close friend. Certainly this is a personal relationship.

Many other immigrant youth imply a personal relationship with God. They speak of worshiping ancestors and having communion with God; they talk about someone who protects them, someone they pray to, someone they can turn to in times of trouble. Across ethnicity and gender, these teenagers who have immigrated to the United States—leaving their homes, their schools, and often their dearest friends behind—carry with them an enduring relationship with a personal God, a God who "is everything to me . . . is all my support."

Discussion and implications

This study reveals the perceived importance of religion in the lives of immigrant youth. In response to two simple questions regarding religion and belief in God, they spoke of real, rich, and powerful personal experiences. The intensity and richness of their responses suggest that religion is perceived to be helpful and meaningful in their lives. The voices of these immigrant youth are strong and powerful, similar to the unforgettable image of the hallway in the dimly lit, run-down building in one of Boston's large housing projects, where *"Dios te ama"* (God loves you) was the simple, repeated message of the bumper sticker stuck over cracks and holes in the walls, and pictures of saints and a large gold cross over the doorway represented the support that came with them on their crossing to a new land.

Interestingly, religion appears to play a less significant role in the lives of Chinese immigrant youth. This perhaps is a reflection of the secular nature of Chinese society under communist rule. For the majority of the Latino immigrants as well as the Haitian youth in our sample, however, religion plays a central role. Although there were significant differences between the three cultural groups, the responses are consistent across genders. This emphasizes the importance of understanding the commonalities across ethnic groups as well as the differences between them.

The process of immigration exposes youth to many stressors, including family dissolution, cultural alienation, racism, a sense of dislocation and disempowerment, loss of familiarity, isolation, and acculturation stress. It is a process in which old relationships are disrupted and new relationships may involve members of an unfamiliar culture. Immigrant youth report multiple ways in which religion or religious belief serves to protect them from the stressors of adolescence and immigration. Participants in our study described a supportive, ever-present relationship with God that protected them from feeling utterly alone or abandoned. The participants

expressed how, when their families suffered separations and dissolution, religious practice supported cohesiveness in the family and
a sense of connection to extended family. Participants reported that
religion provided them with a sense of continuity with familiar cultural practices. Though often residing in urban settings with the
allure of drugs, early sexual activity, and violence, participants
shared how religion offered them a sense of control over their
behavior and a strong boundary between right and wrong. Disen-
franchised from the new culture by racism and language boundaries, immigrant youth often feel disempowered. Participants
report perceiving greater self-efficacy and a sense of attainable help
through prayer or ritual.

Future research should further examine the variety of religious
practices of different ethnic groups. Many immigrant youth, across
the three ethnic groups, made statements distinguishing belief in
God from participation in religious organization. Chinese youth
referred to rituals practiced at home or the celebration of festivals
to worship ancestors, while Latino youth more often described the
ritual of prayer or participation in communion, and Haitians
described participation in Haitian church communities. This study
did not explore specific practices, but this would be an important
area for future study that could inform the implementation of pro-
gramming efforts.

Immigrant youth are becoming an increasingly significant part
of the American population.[21] Policymakers, educators, and those
in other helping fields are realizing the need to foster resilience
and to protect these youth from a myriad of stressors. When considering potential means of fostering resiliency, religion should
not be overlooked. Immigrant youth, particularly Latino and
Haitian youth, report that religion or a belief in God is important to them. For immigrant youth who have already established
relations with a religious center or who have already developed
a faith or belief in a religion, emphasizing the role of religion in
their lives can serve to bolster a naturally and culturally relevant
protective factor. Protective factors that are naturally occurring
are likely to be more effective, easier to foster, and more sustain-

able than interventions imposed from the outside. Having a greater understanding of religious practices and affiliations would allow program designers to embed interventions within existing community organizations or practices that are religiously linked.

Notes

1. Rutter, M. (1990). Psychosocial resilience and protective mechanisms. In J. Rolf, A. S. Masten, D. Cicchetti, K. H. Nuechterlein, & S. Weintraub (Eds.), *Risk and protective factors in the development of psychopathology* (pp. 181–214). New York: Cambridge University Press.

2. Bankston, C. L., & Zhou, M. (1995). Religious participation, ethnic identification, and adaptation of Vietnamese adolescents in an immigrant community. *Sociological Quarterly, 36*(3), 523–534; Seeman, T., Dubin, L. F., & Seeman, M. (2003). Religiosity/spirituality and health: A critical review of the evidence for biological pathways. *American Psychologist, 58*(1), 53–63.

3. Jagers, R., & Mock, L. (1993). Culture and social outcomes among inner-city African American children: An Afrographic exploration. *Journal of Black Psychology, 19,* 391–405.

4. Castex, G. M. (1997). Immigrant children in the United States. In N. K. Phillips and S.L.A. Straussner (Eds.), *Children in the environment: Linking social policy and clinical practice* (pp. 43–60). Springfield, IL: Charles Thomas.

5. Hernandez, D. J., & Charney, E. (Eds.). (1998). *From generation to generation: The health and well-being of children in immigrant families.* Washington, DC: National Academy Press; McCloskey, L. A., Southwick, K., Fernandez-Esquer, M. E., and Locke, C. (1995). The psychological effects of political and domestic violence on Central American and Mexican immigrant mothers and children. *Journal of Community Psychology, 23,* 95–116.

6. Suárez-Orozco, M., & Paez, M. M. (2002). Latinos: The research agenda. In M. Suárez-Orozco and M. M. Paez (Eds.), *Latinos: Remaking America.* Berkeley: University of California Press.

7. Masten, A. S. (2001). Ordinary magic: Resilience processes in development. *American Psychologist, 56*(3), 227–238.

8. Bankston & Zhou (1995); Levitt, P. (2002). Two nations under God? Latino religious life in the U.S. In M. Suárez-Orozco and M. M. Paez. (Eds.), *Latinos: Remaking America.* Berkeley: University of California Press; Miller, W. R., & Thoresen, C. E. (2003). Spirituality, religion, and health. *American Psychologist, 58*(1), 24–35.

9. Gallup Organization (2003, January 14). *Religious awakenings bolster Americans' faith.* Available from http://www.gallup.com

10. Pew Forum on Religion & Public Life (2002). Religion in American public life. Washington, DC: Pew Forum on Religion and Public Life. Available from http://www.pewforum.org

11. Maltby, J., and Day, L. (2003). Religious orientation, religious coping, and appraisals of stress: Assessing primary appraisal factors in relationship between religiosity and psychological well-being. *Personality and Individual*

Differences, 34(7), 1209–1224; Pargament, K. I. (1997). *The psychology of religion and coping: Theory, research and practice.* London: Guilford Press.

12. Loewenthal, K. M. (1995). *Mental health and religion.* London: Chapman Hall.

13. Halpern, R. (1990). Poverty and early childhood parenting: Toward a framework for intervention. *American Journal of Orthopsychiatry, 60,* 6–18; Jagers & Mock (1993).

14. Rutter (1990).

15. Levitt, P. (2002).

16. Harker, K. (2001). Immigrant generation, assimilation and adolescent psychological well-being. *Social Forces, 79*(3), 969–1004.

17. Bankston & Zhou (1995).

18. Cheng, L. R. (1999). Sociocultural adjustment of Chinese American students. In C. Park and M. M.-Y. Chi (Eds.), *Asian-American education: Prospects and challenges.* Westport, CT: Bergin & Garvey.

19. Garcia, J. A. (1986). Caribbean migration to the mainland: A review of adaptive experiences. *Annals of the American Academy of Political and Social Sciences, 487,* 114–127.

20. Argueta-Bernal, G. A. (1990). Stress and stress-related disorders in Hispanics: Biobehavioral approaches to treatment. In F. C. Serafica, A. I. Schwebel, R. K. Russell, P. D. Isaac, and L. B. Myers (Eds.), *Mental Health of Ethnic Minorities.* New York: Praeger.

21. Suárez-Orozco, C., & Suárez-Orozco, M. (2001). *Children of immigration.* Cambridge, Mass.: Harvard University Press.

NORA E. THOMPSON *is a doctoral student in counseling psychology at the School of Education of Boston College.*

ANDREA G. GURNEY *is a doctoral student in counseling and applied educational psychology at Northeastern University and is currently interning at Cambridge Hospital at the Harvard Medical School.*

This chapter draws on longitudinal data to examine the role of gender in immigrant students' educational adaptation. Analyses show that over time girls receive higher grades and express higher future expectations than do boys. Compared with boys, immigrant girls are more likely to be protected from risk factors, such as harsh school environments, by a supported network of teachers, friends, and parents, and to benefit from the shield of ethnicity more than their male counterparts in their pursuit of education.

6

Gendered expectations and gendered experiences: Immigrant students' adaptation in schools

Desirée Baolian Qin-Hilliard

THE LAST FIFTEEN YEARS have witnessed growing scholarly attention to immigrant children's adaptation in the United States.[1] A consistent yet often ignored theme in research on immigrant children's adaptation and mobility is the gender gap in their educational

The author thanks Marcelo Suárez-Orozco and Carola Suárez-Orozco, codirectors of the Harvard Immigration Project, for providing the opportunity for her to develop a focus on gender within the Longitudinal Immigrant Adaptation study; Carola Suárez-Orozco and Irina Todorova for their skillful editing; and Mary Patricia Harmon and Mark Verheyden Hilliard for their comments on an earlier version of this paper.

NEW DIRECTIONS FOR YOUTH DEVELOPMENT, NO. 100, WINTER 2003 © WILEY PERIODICALS, INC.

outcomes. Girls from immigrant families across most ethnic groups tend to have higher educational aspirations and higher educational attainments than their male counterparts. For example, Portes and Rumbaut's study of first- and second-generation immigrant students from diverse ethnic backgrounds finds that girls attain higher grades and have higher educational and professional aspirations than do boys.[2] Brandon's study of Asian high school seniors[3] and Rong and Brown's study of African and Caribbean immigrants[4] find that female students outperformed their male counterparts in school attainments. Other researchers have documented similar gender patterns in their studies of immigrant children.[5]

Few studies, however, have systematically examined why this gender pattern exists. A number of potential factors affecting immigrant girls' adaptation and mobility emerge from the literature. First, researchers have documented the gender role shift after immigration to the United States in many immigrant communities.[6] Parents are more likely to support girls' education here than in their country of origin, because they perceive their daughters' education and future job opportunities as closely linked to the family's sense of "making it" in the United States.[7] Second, ethnographic research has consistently shown that across ethnic groups, immigrant parents place much stricter controls on their daughters than on their sons in their activities outside the house.[8] This heavy parental monitoring may have unanticipated benefits for girls' schooling by minimizing their exposure to violence and toxic environments, particularly in the inner-city context.[9] Third, some researchers find that immigrant girls have a more positive attitude toward school than do boys.[10] This positive attitude may stem from immigrant girls' view of school as a liberating social space where they are free from their parents' heavy monitoring,[11] and their instrumental view of education as "empowerment against tradition"[12]—that is, a good education may give them more leverage in future schooling and marriage. In her recent study of Caribbean youth, Nancy Lopez finds that female students tend to have more positive experiences with teachers. This may also account for immigrant girls' generally positive attitudes toward school.[13] Finally, some researchers find that immigrant girls are less likely to perceive and internalize racism from the dominant society and are less likely than boys to develop an "oppositional relationship" with the educational system.[14]

Nevertheless, few studies have focused specifically on the role of gender in recently arrived immigrant students' educational adaptation. Existing literature tends to focus on the experiences of second-generation students (students born in the United States or who immigrated to the United States at a very young age) or to mix first- and second-generation students in research design. Further, very little research has been conducted using longitudinal data, which may reveal patterns over time that cross-sectional data tend to obscure. Few studies have examined gender differences in recently arrived immigrant students' ethnic identity development over time and how that may relate to their educational outcomes. This is a significant area of inquiry to overlook because a central premise in current research on immigration, education, and mobility argues that ethnicity can facilitate upward mobility—that retaining ethnic culture in the process of adjustment is linked to more positive adaptation.[15]

I address the gap in the literature by providing an initial examination of the role of gender in recently arrived immigrant students' educational adaptation. Drawing on longitudinal data, I explore the following research questions:

Do recently arrived immigrant girls have higher grades and future expectations than do boys? If so, why is this the case?

Do girls and boys have different experiences at school?

Do girls and boys perceive their parents as having different expectations of them?

Are girls more likely to retain their ethnic identity than boys?

Do girls and boys have different adaptation patterns over time?

Method

This study is embedded in the five-year Longitudinal Immigrant Student Adaptation (LISA) study. The sample reported in this chapter consists of 411 recently arrived adolescent immigrant students from Central America, China, the Dominican Republic, Haiti, and Mexico.[16] There are slightly more girls (52 percent, N = 215) than boys (48 percent, N = 215). (Please see Suárez-Orozco and Todorova's introductory chapter for a more detailed description of the Harvard Immigration Project.)

For the purpose of the present study, I use data from annually collected student report cards, annually conducted structured student interviews, and behavioral checklists completed by teachers obtained in 1999 and 2000. I examine the following aspects of students' adaptation: grades, future aspirations, attitudes toward school, time spent on homework, teacher perceptions of student engagement, perceived support at school, peer influences, school safety, parental expectations and control, and ethnic identity (specific measures are presented in the next section). I use T-tests and chi-square tests to detect gender differences.[17] I also report data from open-ended questions in student and teacher interviews to help illustrate certain observed gender patterns.

Findings

Grades

Students' report cards were collected annually from school year 1997–1998 to school year 2001–2002. Grade point average (GPA) is calculated using a five-point scale from 1 to 5, with 5 being the equivalent of A, 4 of B, 3 of C, 2 of D, and 1 of F.[18] Results show that, concurring with the literature, girls in the sample consistently had significantly higher GPAs than the boys throughout the five-year period (see Figure 6.1). It is also important to note that both girls' and boys' grades dropped over time. However, the drop was sharper for the boys. Thus, the gap between girls' and boys' GPAs widened over time from .28 in the third year to .45 in the fourth year, and to more than half a grade (.52) by the fifth year. While in the third year girls had significantly higher average grades than boys only in language arts, by the fourth and fifth years of the study,

Figure 6.1. Comparison of GPA by gender, school year 1997–1998 to school year 2001–2002

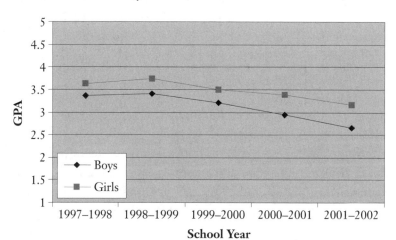

girls had significantly higher grades than the boys in all four sub-jects examined—language arts, math, science, and social studies.

The trend toward a widening of the gender gap in grades held true for Chinese, Dominican, Central American, and particularly Mexican students. While in the first year Mexican boys and girls had similar GPAs—both 3.5—in the fifth year, Mexican girls' GPAs were much higher (3.15) compared to the boys' (2.63). Interest-ingly, for Haitian students, very few gender differences were found except in the second year, when girls' grades were slightly higher than boys'.

Future aspirations

Throughout the interviews, the girls consistently reported higher educational aspirations than did the boys. In the first-year inter-views, 50 percent of the girls reported they wanted to obtain a pro-fessional degree compared to 40 percent of the boys. In the third-, fourth-, and final-year student interviews, girls were significantly more likely than boys to have college plans instead of considering working as their main goal right after high school. For example, in the third-year student interview, 76 percent of the girls reported post high school college plans compared to 64 percent of boys (p < .05). In the fifth year, 88 percent of girls reported college plans compared to 71 percent of boys (p < .05). This gender pattern is particularly pronounced among Dominican and Mexican students. In the final student interview, 91 percent of the Dominican girls and 90 percent of the Mexican girls reported college plans compared to 68 percent of the Dominican boys and 51 percent of the Mexican boys. Overall, the boys were more likely to consider work after high school (25 percent of boys compared to 11 percent of girls). However, there are differences across ethnic groups: 46 percent of Mexican boys and 23 percent of Dominican boys reported that they planned to work right after high school, compared to only 3 percent of Chinese boys.

It is not surprising that the girls also expressed more confidence in their future education than did the boys. In the final student interview, girls were significantly more likely than boys to believe that they would certainly finish high school (80 percent of girls, 60 percent of boys, p < .05) and certainly go to college (56 percent of girls, 47 percent of boys, p < .05).

Attitudes toward school

An index of attitudes toward school is calculated by taking the average of three items on a four-point Likert scale of 1 to 4, with 4 being "very important" and 1 "not important" in the final three of the yearly interviews. Results show that girls consistently reported significantly more positive attitudes toward school than did boys (see Figure 6.2). For example, in the final-year interview, 73 percent of girls believed that it was "very important" for them to get good grades in school compared to 56 percent of boys. Over time, while the girls maintained their positive attitudes, the boys seemed to experience some drop in the final year. Across ethnic groups, Haitian and Dominican girls reported the most positive attitudes toward school. Surprisingly, Chinese boys reported the least positive attitudes toward school. Only 39 percent of Chinese boys (compared to 62 percent of Chinese girls, 85 percent of Haitian

Figure 6.2. Gender differences in attitude toward school, year three to year five

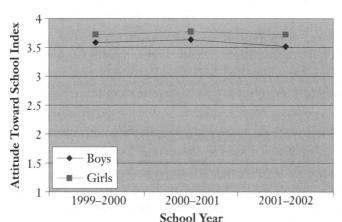

girls, and 84 percent of Dominican girls) considered it very important to get good grades in school.

Time spent on homework

One of the most important factors correlated with educational outcomes is time spent on homework.[19] My analyses show that although in year one there was no gender difference, by year five, girls spent significantly more time on homework every day than did boys—40 percent of girls compared to 19 percent of boys spent more than two hours per day on homework. Across ethnic groups, Chinese girls spent the most time on homework every day, while Mexican students and particularly Dominican boys spent the least time: in year five, 67 percent of Chinese girls (compared to 38 percent of Chinese boys, 16 percent of Mexican girls, 16 percent of Mexican boys, and 0 percent of Dominican boys) spent more than two hours every day doing homework.

Teachers' perception of students' engagement

To better understand students' engagement in school from the teachers' perspective, we asked teachers of three hundred students to fill out student behavioral checklists in the third year. Analyses show that the teachers had overwhelmingly more positive perception of the girls' behaviors and engagement at school than of the boys'. On a scale of 1 to 5, with 1 being "very poor" and 5 "very good," girls received significantly higher ratings from teachers than did boys (see Figure 6.3). Teachers also reported that girls were more likely than boys to finish and turn in homework (p < .05). This is consistent with students' self-reported time on homework. Teachers were also more likely to send boys to the principal's office for behavioral problems (24 percent of boys compared to 11 percent of girls, p < .05). According to teachers, girls also had better teacher and peer relations than did boys. Overall, the teachers perceived girls in a much more positive light than they perceived boys. One teacher's response summarizes well the general outlook of many of her colleagues: "Girls, in general . . . tend to be more willing to buckle down, do their work, get all of their homework in. With boys, lots of times, there is more of a tendency to get distracted, to take as a role some antisocial types of behavior."[20]

Figure 6.3. Comparing gender differences in teachers' perception of student engagement at school: Teachers' ratings of students' engagement being "very good" (N = 300)

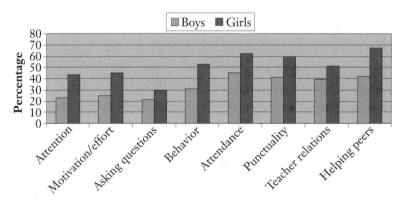

Perceived support at school

As part of the interviews, we asked students to report on their perceived general support from teachers, counselors, and peers at school, measured by the average of eleven items on a four-point Likert scale with 1 being "very true" and 4 being "very false." Results show that girls reported higher levels of support at school than did boys. For example, in the fourth year, 51 percent of girls considered that they could always count on an adult at school compared to 36 percent of boys. Across ethnic groups, Chinese students reported the lowest levels of support at school. Dominican girls reported the most support. For example, in year four, only 10 percent of Chinese boys and 20 percent of Chinese girls said they could talk about their troubles with someone at school compared to 65 percent of Dominican girls. Similarly, 71 percent of the Dominican girls considered that they could count on someone at school (compared to 27 percent of Dominican boys, 24 percent of Chinese boys, and 31 percent of Chinese girls).

Peer influences

Peer influence is another important factor affecting students' educational outcomes. While the majority (87 percent) of both girls and boys had friends from their own ethnic group, girls considered their friends to have significantly more positive attitudes toward school than boys did in the third-year (p < .05) and fourth-year (p < .05) interviews. In the fourth year, 40 percent of girls compared to 26 percent of boys said their friends considered it very important to get good grades in school. Girls also reported significantly more positive support from their friends in school than did boys throughout the final three of the yearly interviews. For example, by the fifth year, 85 percent of girls said that their friends explained things they didn't understand in class, compared to 73 percent of boys. Twenty-three percent of the boys said their friends almost never help them with homework compared to 13 percent of girls. Boys were also more likely to indicate negative influences from their friends. A higher percentage of boys (24 percent) than girls

(18 percent) said that their friends asked them to cut classes. Across ethnic groups, fully 41 percent of Mexican boys and 26 percent of Mexican girls reported that their friends asked them to cut classes. Boys were also more likely to talk about their friends blocking them from doing well in school. For example, a twelve-year-old Dominican boy reported, "Sometimes some of my friends complain and criticize me that I want to do everything perfect. And they don't care if they get an F but I want to always get an A." Similarly, an eleven-year-old Haitian boy said, "Sometimes—like when I'm trying to work, Steven [a friend] bothers me. He always laughs though I don't listen to him. Maybe when I'm reading he does the same thing—always laugh[s] and talk[s]. He is my friend. He always wants to talk to me."

Perception of school safety and ethnic tensions

In the interviews we also asked students about their school environment. While there is no gender difference, these data are quite telling. A significant portion of students depicted their school as a place with violence, gangs, drugs, and ethnic tensions. This was particularly the case for Mexican, Central American, and Dominican participants, who were more likely to be enrolled in inner-city schools. In the third-year interview, 29 percent of boys and 37 percent of girls considered their school to be affected by crime and violence in the community. Close to half of all participants (75 percent of Dominican boys and 64 percent of Mexican boys) felt unsafe at school because of gangs. A third of the students reported seeing fights several times a week or daily, and close to half of the students witnessed bullying several times a week or daily. Over time students felt slightly safer, perhaps because they had habituated to these circumstances. Nevertheless, by the final-year interview, 22 percent of boys and 33 percent of girls still indicated that their school was badly affected by crime and violence, and close to one third of students felt unsafe in school because of gangs.

The students were also concerned about ethnic tensions. Around 75 percent of the participants reported that students from different backgrounds, particularly bilingual and nonbilingual students, did not get along at school. For example, a twelve-year-old Mexican girl said they get along "poorly. They yell a ton of bad words. They are almost always in trouble with the principal. Those who speak English shout out bad words to those who do not speak English." Similarly, a fourteen-year-old Haitian girl said, "They [bilingual and nonbilingual students] don't get along. They lie about one another. They try to put the ones in the other groups down. . . . They [nonbilingual students] make me feel like I should go back to my country. They make me feel like I don't belong here, but I know I'm here for a reason, to get opportunities. It hurts me." Boys also talked about being hurt at school. However, unlike girls, they tended to hide their emotional vulnerability by presenting a tough and cool appearance, what Pollack calls the "mask of masculinity."[21] For example, a sixteen-year-old Haitian boy said, "Some students get along. Others they talk trash, they get into fights. Boys mostly. [It created some problems for me] because some people talk trash to me, especially at the gym or on the basketball court in the school. Sometimes they mean it, sometimes they don't. Even when they're just teasing me, it hurts me but I don't show it. I don't tell them."

Parental expectation and parental monitoring

Parental expectation is another factor affecting students' performance at school. Girls perceived higher educational expectations from their parents than did boys in the first-year interview. A higher percentage of girls (82 percent) than boys (70 percent) reported that their parents considered their going to college "very important" (p < .05). Furthermore, significantly more girls than boys reported that their parents wanted them to continue in their education rather than work after high school (p < .05). This pattern held true for students from all five countries. This is also consistent with the students' own educational expectations reported earlier.

One of the most consistent findings on immigrant girls is the strict parental control of their activities outside home. In the final student interview, a higher percentage of girls (67 percent) than boys (50 percent) reported that their parents always knew their whereabouts. Across ethnic groups both girls and boys believed that girls had much less freedom than boys in dating, spending time with friends, activities outside the house, and finding a part-time job. For example, a fourteen-year-old Central American girl said, "I would have more freedom [if I were a boy]. Because with the men, they [parents] allow them to do as they want. For example, if they go out at night and come back at 3 A.M., they don't tell them anything." Similarly, a thirteen-year-old Dominican girl told us, "It is visible to the naked eye that Hispanic parents are more strict with their daughters than with sons. They watch and control them more. They see everything with them as a problem. For example, they worry if she is too young to go out, if it is getting late and she is not home, if they give her or not permission to go out, etcetera. Instead Americans treat their daughters and sons as equals." Both girls and boys from other ethnic groups echoed these feelings in the interviews.

Ethnic identity

Data for ethnic identity come from answers to the question, "What do you call yourself? That is, what nationality or ethnicity do you consider yourself?" Analyses demonstrate that although in the first year there was no gender difference in ethnic identity—roughly 85 percent of participants adopted country-of-origin identity—in the fifth year there was a significant gender difference ($p < .05$, see Figure 6.4). While the percentage of country-of-origin identity dropped for both girls and boys from the first year to the fifth year, the drop was sharper for boys—from 87 percent to 60 percent (compared to 85 percent to 73 percent for girls). The trend held true for all given ethnic groups, particularly for Dominican, Central American, and Haitian boys. In fact, Central American girls' country-of-origin identity actually went up from 68 percent to 74 percent while Central American boys' dropped from 95 percent to 68 percent. Over time the immigrant boys were more likely than girls to adopt hyphenated identities (such as Chinese-American or Dominican-American)—from 6 percent to 18 percent for boys

Figure 6.4. Percentages of country-of-origin identity by gender and country of origin, year one through year five

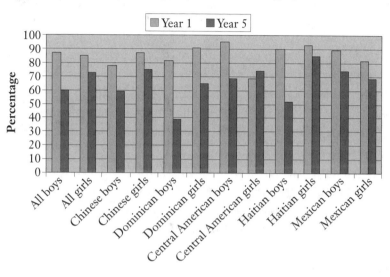

compared to 4 percent in both years for girls. Similar percentages of girls and boys adopted panethnic identities (such as Asian, Latino, or black for Haitian students)—21 percent for boys and 22 percent for girls in year five compared to 6 percent for boys and 11 percent for girls in year one.

Discussion

Earlier research on adolescent and youth development in the United States was based largely on the experiences of white boys.[22] Only recently have researchers started to examine the experiences of girls[23] and minority boys.[24] In the field of developmental psychology, however, very little research has been done to date on the experiences and development of immigrant minority youth. Compared with native-born youth, immigrant youth face more risk factors due to multiple losses and stresses related to immigration, including family separations, loss of extended family and friends, acculturation stress, and language barriers. Identity formation can be particularly challenging for immigrant youth due to the multiple linguistic and cultural worlds they traverse daily as well as to prejudice and discrimination from mainstream society. Furthermore, a large share of immigrant students are trapped in segregated schools infested with urban vices.[25] A large share of participants in this study described the schools they attended as ethnically segregated, with frequent fights, bullying, ethnic tensions, and gang activities.

In this context, findings from this study suggest that the immigrant girls managed to overcome these risk factors in their educational adaptation better than the boys did over time. There is a distinct pattern of widening gap in educational adaptation between genders: girls' advantage in grades grew stronger in the final two years of the study. By the fifth year, the girls were also more academically oriented in their post high school plans and were more confident in their expectations to finish high school and go to college. Boys were more likely than girls to be work-oriented and to become less engaged in schooling (over time they spent significantly less time on homework than did girls). This is particularly true with Dominican and Mexican students, who were more likely to attend segregated urban schools. This implies that the urban realities typical of many schools may have a more negative impact on immigrant boys' educational adaptation than on girls'. This has important implications for their future upward mobility in a society where education is becoming ever more closely linked to future prospects.

Why did the girls do better in school and why were they more academically oriented than the boys over time? Results from this study indicate that immigrant girls may be protected from risk factors like harsh school environment by the supportive network of teachers, peers, and parents they meet in their pursuit of education. Girls had better relations with teachers and more support in school than did boys. Girls had friends who were more serious about schoolwork and more supportive of academics, while boys were more likely to be negatively influenced by their friends. In addition, girls perceived higher expectations in schooling from parents than did boys, and parents also monitored girls more closely than they did the boys.

Researchers have documented that both within and outside the family, social capital can be instrumental in promoting educational outcomes of youth, particularly immigrant minority youth.[26] The immigrant girls in this study had more sources of social capital both within the family, in the form of parental monitoring and parental expectation, and outside the family, in the form of peer networks and teacher support. This helps them to achieve their educational goals despite the risk factors.

The immigrant boys, however, had fewer sources of social capital either within or outside the family. For them, this protective network of supportive relations was weaker. At home, parents gave them more freedom to date, be with friends, and be on the street. As a result, it may have been easier for them to be distracted from school, because unlike girls, they had more alternatives. Lack of parental supervision increased the opportunities for their exposure to negative influences on the street, such as gangs and drugs. Furthermore, as Connell argues, for many minority boys attending urban schools, their construction of a masculine identity was likely to be in conflict with the school agenda.[27] For immigrant minority boys, their construction of a gender identity was closely linked to their racial and ethnic identity. To be respected among their peers, immigrant minority boys often had to present and emphasize their masculinity at school by acting cool and tough. As a result, teachers, mostly female, may have been likely to perceive immigrant minority boys as having more behavioral problems than girls and likely to view them as more threatening and dangerous than immigrant girls, which may have led them to punish boys more severely. This had a potentially negative impact on their development.

Implications

An implication of this study is that ethnic identity may play an important role in immigrant students' gender gap in educational adaptation. Corresponding to the drop in grades being sharper for boys, the drop of country-of-origin identification was also sharper for boys.

Hence, boys appeared to be assimilating more quickly than girls were. This may be due to the influence of parents and peers. Girls who are monitored more strictly by their parents tend to spend more time at home and to maintain more of their ethnic culture through their parents. Boys who spend time with their friends on the street have more opportunities than girls to be exposed to and to assimilate into the prevalent culture, which is often that of the inner city. For many immigrant students today, daily exposure and assimilation into urban school and neighborhood environments may lead to downward social mobility. For these students, ethnicity—that is maintaining native culture and language—may play a protective role, shielding them from the negative influences of today's urban America. In regard to their education, immigrant girls appear to benefit from this shield of ethnicity more than their male counterparts.

It is important for educators and other professionals working with immigrant students, particularly those in inner-city schools, to be aware that maintaining this shield of ethnicity is positively linked to favorable academic adaptation. They should encourage immigrant students to retain their culture and language while learning English and to adapt to school and the new culture. Boys may face greater challenges in this process.

It is also important for researchers, practitioners, and policymakers working with immigrant populations to be aware of gender differences in students' adaptation. More supportive after-school programs and mentoring programs can help immigrant boys as well as girls to maintain their focus on school.[28] Immigrant community organizations can also play a very important role by providing a space after school for students to study and by ensuring meaningful activities in which students may interact with peers in a healthy and cognitively stimulating environment.[29]

Finally, this study also points to the importance of creating a healthier school environment for immigrant students. At school, bilingualism and immigration experiences are often seen as negative and undesirable. Ethnic tension and prejudices against immigrant students have a very negative impact on their development.

It is important for educators to create a healthy school environment where cultural and linguistic differences can be understood from different and more positive perspectives and be integrated into the general school curriculum. This is particularly important considering the globalization processes taking place in the world today. Large-scale immigration will continue, with the world becoming more global at the demographic, economic, technological, and cultural levels. One of the most important implications of globalization for education is the need to nurture students' abilities and sensibilities to interact and work with those who come from different linguistic and cultural backgrounds.[30] Creating a healthy school environment where students from different backgrounds can interact positively will promote the development of all children, both girls and boys, natives and immigrants alike.

Notes

1. Suárez-Orozco, C., & Suárez-Orozco, M. (2001). *Children of immigration*. Cambridge, MA: Harvard University Press; Gibson, M. A. (1988). *Accommodation without assimilation: Sikh immigrants in an American high school*. Ithaca and London: Cornell University Press; Olsen, L. (1997). *Made in America: Immigrant students in our public schools*. New York: New Press.

2. Portes, A., & Rumbaut, R. G. (2001). *Legacies: The story of the second generation*. Berkeley: University of California Press.

3. Brandon, P. (1991). Gender differences in young Asian Americans' educational attainment. *Sex Roles 25*(1/2), 45–61.

4. Rong, X. L., and Brown, F. (2001). The effects of immigrant generation and ethnicity on educational attainment among young African and Caribbean Blacks in the United States. *Harvard Educational Review, 71*(3), 536–565.

5. Olsen (1997); Waters, M. (1996). The intersection of gender, race, and ethnicity in identity development of Caribbean American teens. In B.J.R. Leadbeater and N. Way (Eds.), *Urban girls: Resisting stereotypes, creating identities* (pp. 65–84). New York: New York University Press.

6. Hondagneu-Sotelo, P. (1992). Overcoming patriarchal constraints: The reconstruction of gender relations among Mexican immigrant women and men. *Gender and Society, 6*, 393–415; Zhou, M. (1992). *Chinatown*. Philadelphia: Temple University Press.

7. Olsen (1997).

8. Waters (1996); Sarroub, L. K. (2001). The sojourner experience of Yemeni American high school students: An ethnographic portrait. *Harvard Educational Review, 71*(3), 390–415.

9. Smith, R. C. (2002). Gender, ethnicity, and race in school and work outcomes of second-generation Mexican Americans. In M. Suárez-Orozco and M. M. Paez (Eds.), *Latinos Remaking America.* Berkeley: University of California Press.

10. Sarroub (2001); and Waters (1996).

11. Olsen (1997).

12. Keaton, T. (1999). Muslim girls and the "other France": An examination of identity construction. *Social Identities, 5*(1), 47–64.

13. Lopez, N. (2003). *Hopeful girls, troubled boys: Race and gender disparity in urban education.* New York: Routledge.

14. Waters (1996); Rumbaut, R. G. (1996). The crucible within: Ethnic identity, self-esteem, and segmented assimilation among children of immigrants. In A. Portes (Ed.), *The New Second Generation.* New York: Russell Sage Foundation; Waters, M. (1999). *Black identities: West Indian dreams and American realities.* Cambridge, MA: Harvard University Press.

15. Portes, A., and Zhou, M. (1993). The new second generation: Segmented assimilation and its variants. *Annals of the American Academy of Political & Social Science, 530,* 74–96; Portes & Rumbaut, 2001.

16. 411 is the number of participants in the first year. Attribution was roughly 5 percent each year.

17. The measure of statistical significance is a probability level of .05 throughout the chapter.

18. Different schools used different grading systems. We found five grading systems across the participating schools and converted them all to a numeric scale from 1 to 5.

19. Portes & Rumbaut, 2001.

20. See also Suárez-Orozco, C., and Qin-Hilliard, D. B. (forthcoming). The cultural psychology of academic engagement: Immigrant boys' experiences in U.S. schools. In N. Way and J. Chu (Eds.), *Adolescent boys in context.* New York: New York University Press.

21. Pollack, W. (1998). *Real boys: Rescuing our sons from the myths of boyhood.* New York: Holt.

22. Erikson, E. (1968). *Identity: Youth and Crisis.* New York: Norton.

23. Gilligan, C. (1982). *In a different voice.* Cambridge, MA: Harvard University Press; Brown, L., and Gilligan, C. (1992). *Meeting at the crossroads: Women's psychology and girls' development.* New York: Ballantine Books.

24. Hudson, R. J. (1991). Black male adolescent development deviating from the past: Challenges for the future. In B. P. Bowser (Ed.), *Black male adolescents: Parenting and education in community context.* Lanham, MD: University Press of America.

25. Suárez-Orozco & Suárez-Orozco (2001). For school segregation, see Orfield, G., and Yun, J. T. (1999). Resegregation in American schools. Cambridge, MA: Civil Rights Project, Harvard University.

26. See Goyette, K., & Conchas, G. Q. (2002). Family and nonfamily roots of social capital among Vietnamese and Mexican children. In B. Fuller & E. Hannum (Eds.), *Schooling and social capital in diverse cultures* (pp. 41–71). Oxford: JAI.

27. Connell, R. W. (2000). Teaching boys. In *The men and the boys.* Berkeley: University of California Press.

28. Rhodes, J., Grossman, J. B., & Resch, N. L. (2000). Agents of change: Pathways through which mentoring relationships influence adolescents' academic adjustment. *Child Development,* 71(6), 1662–1671.

29. Zhou & Li, this volume.

30. Suárez-Orozco, M. and Qin-Hilliard, D. B. (Eds.) (Forthcoming) *Globalization: Culture and education in the new millennium.* Berkeley: University of California Press.

DESIRÉE BAOLIAN QIN-HILLIARD *is a doctoral student in human development and psychology at the Harvard Graduate School of Education.*

This chapter uses data from the Longitudinal Immigrant Student Adaptation Study to examine media use patterns among immigrant teens. Similarities and differences in media ownership levels, use patterns, and content preferences between immigrant teens and the U.S. teen population as a whole, as well as across immigrant groups and gender, are explored. Implications for educators and others who work with immigrant youth include active discussion with youth about their media choices and media messages.

7

Media in the lives of immigrant youth

Josephine Louie

YOUTH IN THE United States today live in a world filled with a variety of communications media. Most youth are exposed to a diversity of traditional print media, such as books, newspapers, and magazines, both inside and outside of their homes. Increasingly, U.S. teens are likely to have multiple TV sets in their homes, and more are gaining access to VCRs, DVDs, and computerized devices that can record and play television or other video programs at any hour of the day. Music popular with young people can come from traditional sources such as radios and tape players, or from newer channels such as minidiscs or portable, handheld sound machines that play music files downloaded from the Web. Homework assignments issued by schools increasingly involve research

NEW DIRECTIONS FOR YOUTH DEVELOPMENT, NO. 100, WINTER 2003 © WILEY PERIODICALS, INC.

conducted on the Internet and written outputs produced and submitted through a computer. The range of communication media available to young people is rich, wide, and likely to continue to increase in the future.

As the number and variety of media have increased across U.S. households, media use among young people has become more private and independent. Almost two-thirds of American youth between the ages of fourteen and eighteen have a TV in their bedroom; about 90 percent have a CD player, tape player, or radio; more than 40 percent have a video device and a video game player; and almost 20 percent have a computer in their room.[1] Greater media independence enhances youths' abilities to access information free from the knowledge and supervision of parents and other adults.[2]

Regular access to information through media raises questions about the media content that young people consume and about how such content may shape their social views and behaviors. Indeed, media researchers have long recognized that media may play an important role in the socialization of youth. Some argue that "the evidence is so ample that few mass communication scholars hesitate to list mass media as equal in importance to most other socialization agents (e.g., parents, schools, churches) in the lives of contemporary U.S. children."[3]

Most scholars agree that information gained from the media may have its greatest impact when other sources of information on these topics are limited or unavailable. For instance, adolescent youth may be highly influenced by television content or popular music lyrics on sex and male-female relationships if adults or other people in youths' lives do not discuss these topics or address their questions.[4] Researchers have observed that children who view and discuss television with adults can take away from the medium different messages than do those who watch alone.[5] Children have been found to be more likely to imitate aggressive behavior seen on television if an adult observer comments positively on the portrayal than if the adult makes negative comments.[6] While media may offer young people exposure to a wide range of ideas and social behaviors, the beliefs that youth adopt and how they act on media content are often mediated in turn by the people and social conditions around them.

The media and immigrant youth

National media surveys suggest that subgroups of U.S. youth display distinct media ownership and media use patterns. For instance, youth from households with lower incomes and lower levels of education have been found to own fewer computers but they own and watch more television than their peers. African Americans and Hispanics have been found to watch more television than white Americans; this finding holds for African Americans even at higher income levels.[7] Little prior research has been performed on the media use patterns of immigrant youth. Because these youth are a distinct subpopulation of the country, and because many join the United States as racial and ethnic minorities, it is likely that they will exhibit media consumption patterns different from those of nonimmigrant, majority youth.

Many immigrant youth come to the United States with fewer economic resources than those in the dominant society. Some may therefore display media ownership patterns common to youth from families with lower incomes in this country. At the same time, immigrant youth have media options that may not be accessible to majority youth. Latinos in the United States can choose from an increasing array of Spanish-language television channels, radio stations, and print media providing ethnic content.[8] Chinese-language television channels, videotaped programs, radio stations, and newspapers are becoming more prevalent in areas of the country with large numbers of Chinese immigrants.[9] Ethnic language media may offer to immigrant youth information and entertainment options that can substitute for or supplement mainstream U.S. media channels.

Immigrant youth may also display distinct media use patterns because of their special needs and interests as newcomers to the country. Feelings of social disorientation and isolation are common among people who leave their native culture and join a new society. Newly arrived immigrants may turn to host society media for a sense of companionship or to acquire information about the behavioral norms and social expectations of their new country.[10] Immigrant youth may rely heavily on media such as American television, film, or radio to learn English as well as the standards of American youth culture—especially if they are surrounded by parents or coethnic peers who cannot help them build such knowledge.

Little is known about the media that immigrant youth consume and about how these media may shape their understandings of themselves and their new country. Some studies have explored media use and media effects among racial and ethnic minorities in the United States, but many studies were performed several decades ago and have focused primarily on African Americans. To begin to understand the role that media may play in the lives of today's immigrant youth, we need a basic picture of the types of media these youth consume, and of whether patterns vary across different immigrant groups. This study is an effort to develop such a picture.

Methods

The data in this study were collected as part of the Longitudinal Immigrant Student Adaptation (LISA) Study conducted at Harvard University, which included adolescents from China, Haiti, the Dominican Republic, Central America, and Mexico.[11] (Please see Chapter One of this volume by Suárez-Orozco and Todorova for a more detailed description of the Harvard Immigration Project.) Data on media ownership within the home, media exposure levels, and media content preferences were collected from youth in the spring of 2002. Questions probing students' media ownership and exposure levels were adapted from questions posed in a national media use survey conducted in 1999 by Roberts, Foehr, Rideout, and Brodie for the Kaiser Family Foundation.[12]

Immigrant youth were asked to describe the media environments within their homes, including the number of audiovisual media devices they have and the social contexts surrounding their media use. In addition, the youth reported their levels of exposure to various media during the week, as well as their content and genre preferences within each medium. Participant responses to open-ended questions on media content preferences were translated into English when necessary and coded into media genre categories adapted from those used in the study by Roberts and colleagues. Summary descriptive statistics were calculated for the immigrant sample as a whole, as well as by immigrant group and gender.

Results

The media environment of immigrant youth

Data from the LISA sample suggest that the levels of media ownership within immigrant youth homes are similar to levels found for the U.S. youth population as a whole. Immigrant youth reported an average of 3.5 audio devices (such as radios and tape or CD players) within their homes, followed by 3 TV sets, 2.4 video players (including VCRs and VCD or DVD players), 1.3 videogame players, and 1.1 computers per home. In 1999, Roberts and colleagues found more than 3 radios, almost 3 television sets, about 2 VCRs, 1.4 videogame players, and 1 computer in the home of the average U.S. youth between the ages of two and eighteen. About three-quarters of both the U.S. youth population and the LISA sample have cable or satellite TV service in the home. While just under half of U.S. youth reported having Internet access in 1999, about 62 percent of the immigrant youth sample reported having such access in 2002.

The contexts in which youth use media form an important component of their media environment. Results from the LISA study show that significant shares of immigrant youth have private access to various forms of media within the home (Table 7.1). These shares are comparable to those found for the U.S. youth population as a whole, although a relatively large share of immigrant teens (46 percent) report having a computer in the bedroom.

Table 7.1 also shows that overall trends for the whole sample mask differences across immigrant groups. Interestingly, less than a third of Chinese immigrant teens report having a TV set in the bedroom, compared to roughly 75 percent of the Dominican, Central American, and Mexican teens. On the other hand, Chinese youth are more likely than other groups to have private access to a computer. These patterns are consistent with group differences in media ownership and access within immigrant homes in general: Chinese youth report fewer TV sets and more computers in the home than other groups. Under half of Chinese immigrant youth (46 percent) report having cable or satellite TV in the home, compared to 98 percent of Dominican and 92 percent of Central American youth; and while half or less of Haitian and Mexican teens have Internet access at home, 94 percent of Chinese youth have such access.

Although large shares of immigrant youth have potentially private access to a variety of media in their bedrooms, the vast major-

Table 7.1. Access to private media within the home: Percentage of youth with media in the bedroom

	Total immigrant sample N = 303	Chinese N = 71	Haitian N = 58	Dominican N = 57	Central American N = 48	Mexican N = 69
Audio media (radios and tape/CD players)	84	85	80	79	89	87
TVs	63	32	67	71	75	76
Video game players	47	28	54	56	51	48
Computers	46	61	17	51	53	49
VCRs, VCDs, DVDs	39	25	28	47	54	41

ity of them are likely to use media in the company of others. About one in five immigrant youth watch television "mainly alone," and less than 3 percent watch "always alone" (see Table 7.2). When youth watch TV with others, over half say they watch with siblings, and 42 percent report they watch with their parents. In contrast, national survey data collected by Roberts et al. indicate that one in three U.S. teens between the ages of fourteen and eighteen watch TV "mainly alone," and less than a quarter of teens watch television with their parents. These data suggest that the average immigrant teen may be more likely to watch television with others—especially parents—than the average U.S. teen. This likelihood is especially strong for the Dominicans and Chinese (see Table 7.2).

Media exposure levels

Immigrant youth reported how much time they spent using different media the previous weekday. Their responses mirror patterns for the U.S. youth population as a whole. The average immigrant youth in the LISA sample spends almost two hours each weekday watching TV, more than an hour listening to the radio, more than forty-five minutes listening to music on CDs or tapes and using the computer, and thirty-five minutes or less watching videotapes, reading books, playing video games, or reading magazines (see Figure 7.1). Similarly, the average U.S. teen spends most of his or her media-use time watching television and listening to music.[13]

Table 7.2. Social contexts of television viewing

	Total immigrant sample N = 293	Chinese N = 62	Haitian N = 47	Dominican N = 58	Central American N = 58	Mexican N = 68
Percentage of youth who watch TV						
Mainly alone	21	31	15	36	12	10
Always alone	3	8	0	4	2	3
When youth watch TV with others, percentage who watch with						
Parents	42	45	32	56	30	44
Siblings	58	39	66	75	56	59
Peers	22	23	21	23	28	16

Figure 7.1. Exposure levels to various media: Average time spent using media on the previous day, by immigrant group (hours:minutes)

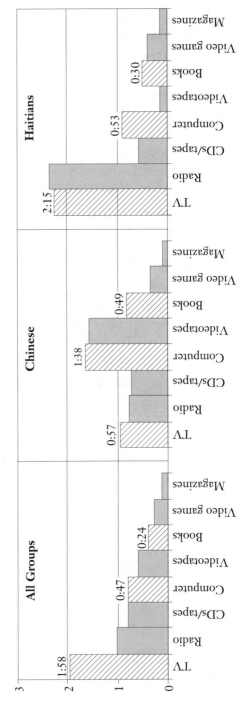

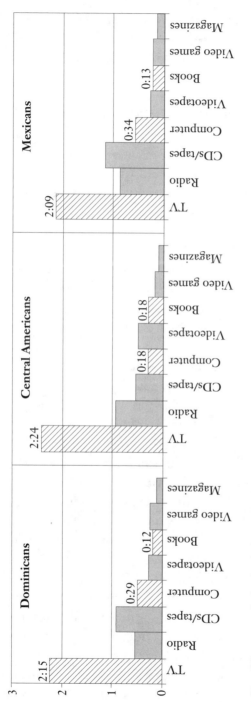

Note: Figures are calculated only for youth who reported media use on a weekday.

Behind these aggregate trends lie differences in media exposure across immigrant groups. Chinese youth on average spend half as much time watching television as other groups do, but at least three times as much time watching videotapes than the others (see Figure 7.1). The Chinese youth also spend more than an hour and a half using the computer and almost fifty minutes reading books each weekday. In contrast, the Haitians report using the computer for less than an hour and reading books for thirty minutes each weekday; the Latino groups report using the computer for about half an hour or less and reading books for less than twenty minutes each weekday.

Media content preferences

The diverse immigrant groups in this study reported different preferences for English-language versus native-language media. The data suggest that immigrant teens display very different media language preferences across regions of origin. The Latino youth (Dominicans, Central Americans, and Mexicans) have a strong preference for the Spanish language when consuming a variety of media: high shares watch television, listen to the radio, and communicate with others on the computer at least half the time in Spanish (see Figure 7.2). In contrast, Chinese immigrant teens typically watch TV, listen to the radio, and communicate on the computer primarily in English, while large shares watch videotapes and read magazines in Chinese half the time or more. Haitian immigrant teens consume almost all media primarily in English.

Immigrant teens also display different genre preferences by group and by medium. The most popular TV programs among Dominicans, Central Americans, and Mexicans are Spanish-language *telenovelas* or soap operas—more than 60 percent of each of these groups regularly watch these dramas. Substantial shares of the Latino teens also like to watch American comedies and American music videos. In contrast, the most popular TV programs among Chinese immigrant teens are American news and children's programs (including cartoons), with a third reporting that they usually watch each of these types of programs. Next most popular among Chinese teens are American comedies and Chinese language dramas or soap operas. About half of Haitian teens say they

**Figure 7.2. Language preferences for various media:
Percentage of youth who use media in English
vs. language of origin (L/O)**

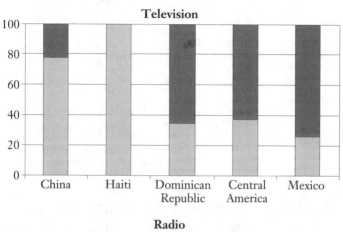

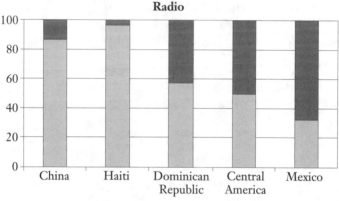

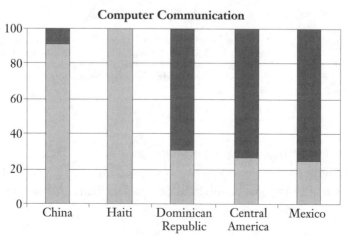

Figure 7.2 *(continued)*

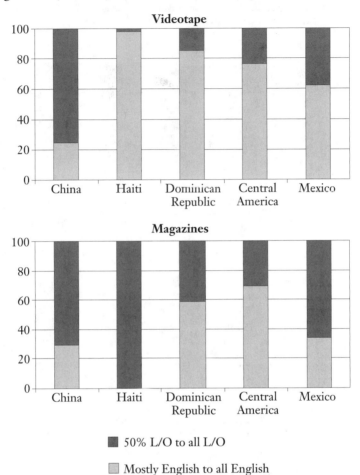

Note: Youth responded to questions with the following general format: "When you use
_____, what language is it usually in?" Five responses were possible: English, mostly
English–some L/O, 50–50, mostly L/O–some English, L/O. The charts above combine the five possible responses into two broader categories. Percentages are calculated for youth who use the medium.

typically watch comedies targeted to black U.S. audiences, while other popular TV programs for this group include comedies targeted to the general public, children's programs and cartoons, movies, and music videos.

Music preferences differ across immigrant groups as well, revealing teen affinities for music linked to their own or related ethnic groups. National media surveys show that U.S. teens in seventh to twelfth grade listen in greatest shares to rap or hip hop music (53 percent) and alternative rock (42 percent). In contrast, almost 90 percent of Haitian youth say they regularly listen to rap or hip hop; more than half report listening to rhythm and blues or "slow jam" music; a third typically listen to reggae or Caribbean music; and none report listening to alternative music. The Latino groups listen in substantial shares to both English and Spanish-language music: more than half of each group listens regularly to rap or hip hop music, while 70 percent of Dominicans listen to salsa and *merengue*, 40 percent of Mexican youth listen to *rancheras* or other forms of Mexican music, and close to a third of Central Americans regularly listen to salsa as well as Spanish-language ballads. Chinese immigrant teens display still different music preferences: almost 70 percent of Chinese teens listen frequently to music in Chinese, Japanese, or Korean performed by pop musicians from Asia, and about 60 percent of these youth listen to Top-40 rock in English.

Gender differences in media use among immigrant teens

Data from the LISA study suggest that immigrant boys and girls have different levels of media access, and they choose and use media in distinct ways. Immigrant boys are significantly more likely than immigrant girls to have a TV set in the bedroom (70 percent versus 57 percent), as well as a video player (46 percent versus 31 percent) and a video game player (56 percent versus 13 percent). These differences contrast with trends for the U.S. youth population as a whole. While U.S. boys aged two to eighteen are more likely than U.S. girls of the same age to have a video game player in the bedroom (43 percent versus 23 percent), U.S. boys are typically no more likely than U.S. girls to have other types of media in the bedroom.[14]

Corresponding to these different media access levels, a significantly larger share of immigrant boys (27 percent) than immigrant girls (15 percent) watch television "mainly alone." While both genders are equally likely to watch television with siblings or friends, immigrant girls are significantly more likely than immigrant boys to watch TV with their parents (46 percent versus 36 percent). Interestingly, immigrant boys and girls display few differences in the amount of time they spend each day watching TV, listening to music, using video players, and using the computer; immigrant boys, however, spend significantly more time than girls playing video games (thirty-four minutes versus three minutes per weekday), and immigrant girls spend significantly more time than boys reading books (thirty minutes versus eighteen minutes per weekday).

Gender differences also emerge in the types of media content that immigrant youth consume. Following trends found within the U.S. youth population at large, immigrant girls are significantly more likely than their male peers to read teen, women's, and entertainment or celebrity magazines, while immigrant boys are more likely to read sports, news, video game, and car and mechanic magazines. Immigrant girls are significantly more likely to do schoolwork and communicate with others on the computer, while immigrant boys are more likely to use the computer to play video games. Finally, language preferences appear to vary by gender—both across different media and within immigrant groups. Latina girls watch Spanish TV, listen to Spanish music, and read Spanish magazines in significantly larger shares than Latino boys (see Figure 7.3). Latino boys display a slight preference over Latina girls for English TV, music, and magazines, although the difference is only statistically significant for magazines. Chinese immigrant girls listen to Asian popular music and read Asian magazines in significantly larger shares than Chinese immigrant boys. There were no gender differences in media language preferences among the Haitian teens since most consume media primarily in English.

Discussion

Results from this study suggest a number of conclusions. First, immigrant teens are very similar to other U.S. teens in many of their media use patterns. Both immigrant teens and teens surveyed

Figure 7.3. Language preferences by medium and gender for Latino and Chinese immigrant youth: Percentage of youth who typically consume media in English or their language of origin

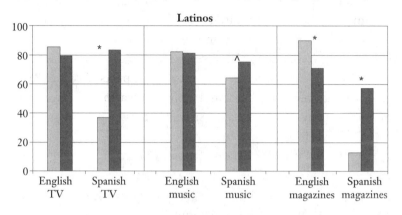

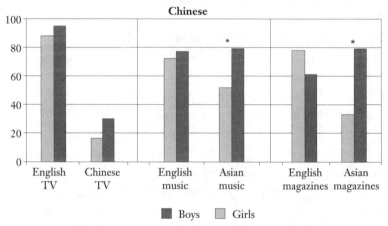

Note: ^ indicates difference is significant at p < 0.10; * indicates p < .05.

from a national sample report comparable numbers of audiovisual media devices in the home and bedroom. Immigrant teens watch many of the same comedy and music television programs, listen to many of the same songs, and peruse many of the same gender-specific magazines as nonimmigrant U.S. teens. Popular television entertainment, music, and magazines often address many of the primary concerns that teens face (such as establishing relationships with one's peers; learning about love, sex, and beauty; and negotiating with authority).[15] Like other adolescent youth, immigrant teens may turn to these media sources to learn not only how to become an adult in the United States, but also how to become a man or woman within American society.

The data in this study also reveal that immigrant teens are dissimilar to other U.S. teens in numerous respects. For instance, teens with immigrant backgrounds appear to watch TV more often in the company of siblings and parents. This use pattern suggests that the impacts and experience of media use could differ between immigrant and other U.S. teens, because the type of content one consumes and the meanings one derives from media are often influenced by the values and behaviors of those in the surrounding context. More needs to be learned about the types of media content immigrant teens consume, discuss, and retain compared to other U.S. youth, as well as what they consume when they are by themselves compared to what they consume when they are with others.

In addition, high shares of some immigrant youth groups choose both ethnic as well as English-language media. Ethnic media could offer comfort and familiarity to immigrant teens who may still have difficulty with English and who may retain cultural values and perspectives from their region of origin. Alternatively, using ethnic media may serve social or family functions. Watching Spanish language or Chinese TV may provide youth with an opportunity to spend time with immigrant parents or other family members who continue to choose ethnic media due to their own language or cultural barriers. Another possible explanation might be developmental: psychologists argue that racial and ethnic minority youth in adolescence face the complicated task of forming a secure sense of their racial or ethnic identity in the United States.[16] Ethnic media may offer opportunities to immigrant youth to learn what it may mean to be a Latino, Haitian, or Chinese person, just as English language media may provide youth with information on what it means to be an American.

Further, not all immigrant teens are alike. Chinese immigrant teens own fewer television sets and more computers and have higher levels of Internet access than other immigrant groups. Correspondingly, these youth spend less time watching TV and more time using the computer than other groups; they also spend more minutes per day reading books. The media ownership and consumption patterns of Chinese youth mirror patterns displayed within the United States among youth from families with higher levels of income and parental education. Future analysis of the LISA data will explore whether the Chinese group's distinct ownership and media use patterns remain after controlling for parental socioeconomic status.

The Haitian teens listen extensively to radio and prefer music and television featuring African American performers. The Dominicans, Central Americans, and Mexican youth gravitate heavily toward Spanish-language media. It is not clear why these Latino groups display a stronger ethnic-language preference than the Chinese and the Haitians, but the trend may partly reflect different levels of ethnic media availability across ethnic groups and U.S. regions. Although Chinese language media outlets have been growing in recent decades,[17] Spanish language television and other media have a longer history in the United States and a wider geographic scope.[18] Compared to the Dominicans, smaller shares of Central Americans and Mexicans report that they regularly watch English-language TV programs; this difference may signal different levels of access to Spanish media between the Northeast and the West coasts.[19]

Immigrant girls from Spanish-speaking countries and China display a greater preference for ethnic media than immigrant boys. This difference could reflect differential pressures on boys and girls to acculturate to U.S. society or to maintain ties with their ethnic heritage. Immigrant girls may experience greater supervision than boys from their parents over their social activities as well as media exposure; indeed, immigrant parents appear to allow greater levels of private media access within the bedroom to boys than to girls. One consequence of this disparity may be that immigrant girls have fewer opportunities to explore English-language media. Alternatively, girls may spend more time at home, closer to their immigrant parents; such proximity may lead indirectly to greater ethnic media consumption if their parents primarily use such media. Further research is required to examine the factors that may contribute to different ethnic media preferences across gender.

Implications

These findings suggest a variety of implications for practitioners working with immigrant youth. Immigrant teens—especially boys—consume significant amounts of English-language media. While some immigrant parents and family members may be able to discuss issues of interest that emerge for youth from ethnic media, educators and counselors native to the United States may be better equipped to ask immigrant youth about the English-language media content they encounter, to address questions about this content, and to discuss the values and behaviors young people may have observed from the media. As adults who can play an important role in mediating the messages of mass media, educators should recognize the substantial presence of media in youths' lives, and they may wish to nurture their own abilities in evaluating media content. Educators who help youth develop a thoughtful and analytic eye toward English media content may equip these youth with media literacy skills that immigrant teens can then bring to their ethnic media consumption.[20]

Because some immigrant teens—especially Latina and Chinese girls—consume significant amounts of ethnic language media, people who work with youth may wish to become more familiar with the content of these media in order to better understand the ideas and values these youth encounter. With this information, youth service providers may be able to spark conversations about social views and behaviors that are directly relevant to youths' everyday experiences—both to gain insight into the issues that may be important to young people and to introduce and explore multiple viewpoints. Knowledge of immigrant youths' detailed media content preferences (in both English and language of origin) may help teachers create lessons that engage youths' existing understandings and interests by drawing on their current home and leisure activities. Such knowledge may also help educators select existing media materials that can be used for educational purposes and that will be compelling to youth.

These findings also suggest a role for people who work with immigrant parents. Parents can serve as "gatekeepers" to children's media, either by directly controlling the media that their children consume or by influencing youths' consumption patterns through their own media choices.[21] Educators can help parents become more aware of their abilities to influence young people's media exposure and interpretations of media content. Encouraging parents to talk with youth about media messages may help youth evaluate media content within broader perspectives. In sum, the mass media may serve as an influential agent of socialization and acculturation in the lives of immigrant youth; at the same time, parents and other adults who explore the media content that youth seek and who are willing to discuss with them the messages they glean may have a powerful impact on the media's ultimate effects.

Notes

1. Roberts, D. F., Foehr, U. G., Rideout, V. J., & Brodie, M. (1999). *Kids and media at the new millennium.* Menlo Park, CA: Henry J. Kaiser Family Foundation.
2. Roberts, Foehr, Rideout, & Brodie (1999).
3. Roberts, Foehr, Rideout, & Brodie (1999), p. 1.
4. Christenson, P. G., & Roberts, D. F. (1998). *It's not only rock and roll: Popular music in the lives of adolescents.* Cresskill, NJ: Hampton Press.
5. Van Evra, J. (1998). *Television and child development* (2nd ed.). Mahwah, NJ: Erlbaum.
6. Comstock, G., & Cobbey, R. E. (1982). Television and the children of ethnic minorities: Perspectives from research. In G. L. Berry & C. Mitchell-Kernan (Eds.), *Television and the socialization of the minority child.* New York: Academic Press.
7. Graves, S. B. (1993). Television, the portrayal of African Americans, and the development of children's attitudes. In G. L. Berry & J. K. Asamen (Eds.), *Children and television: Images in a changing sociocultural world.* Newbury Park: Sage; Roberts, Foehr, Rideout, & Brodie (1999).
8. Subervi-Velez, F., & Colsant, S. (1993). The television worlds of Latino children. In G. L. Berry & J. K. Asamen (Eds.), *Children and television: Images in a changing sociocultural world.* Newbury Park: Sage.

9. Zhou, M., & Cai, G. (2002). Chinese language media in the United States: Immigration and assimilation in American life. *Qualitative Sociology, 25*(3), 419–441.

10. Palmer, E. L., Smith, K. T., & Strawser, K. S. (1993). Rubik's tube: Developing a child's television worldview. In G. L. Berry & J. K. Asamen (Eds.), *Children and television: Images in a changing sociocultural world.* Newbury Park: Sage; Zohoori, A. R. (1988). A cross-cultural analysis of children's television use. *Journal of Broadcasting and Electronic Media, 32*(1), 105–113.

11. I thank Marcelo and Carola Suárez-Orozco, codirectors of the Harvard Immigration Projects, for allowing me to explore media use patterns among immigrant youth within the LISA study.

12. Roberts, Foehr, Rideout, & Brodie (1999).

13. National survey data show that the average youth age fourteen to eighteen in the United States watches two and three-quarter hours of television each day, followed by an hour and a half of listening to CDs or tapes, more than an hour of listening to radio, thirty-seven minutes of reading print media, thirty minutes using the computer, twenty-nine minutes of watching commercial videotapes, and twenty-nine minutes of playing video games (Roberts, Foehr, Rideout, & Brodie, 1999).

14. Roberts, Foehr, Rideout, & Brodie (1999).

15. Christenson & Roberts (1998).

16. Phinney, J. S., & Rosenthal, D. A. (1992). Ethnic identity in adolescence: Process, context, and outcome. In G. R. Adams, T. P. Gulotta, & R. Motemayor (Eds.), *Adolescent identity formation.* Newbury Park, CA: Sage; Phinney, J. S. (1990). Ethnic identity in adolescents and adults: Review of research. *Psychological Bulletin, 108*(3), 499–514.

17. Zhou & Cai (2002).

18. Subervi-Velez & Colsant (1993).

19. All of the Central American and Mexican youth in the LISA study were living in San Francisco, while all the Dominican youth were living in the Boston area.

20. Cortes, C. E. (2000). *The children are watching: How the media teach about diversity* (New York: Teachers College Press). Cortes suggests that educators can respond in multiple ways to the mass media's large presence in the lives of youth. The most basic response is to recognize that teaching and learning occur when youth consume media. Another response is to pay attention to the lessons that media may be promoting. A third response is to seek media materials that can be brought into youth settings for pedagogical purposes. Alongside these responses, educators can work to develop students' as well as their own analytical thinking about media content (pp. 135–145).

21. Cortes (2000), p. 24.

JOSEPHINE LOUIE *is a doctoral student in administration, planning, and social policy at the Harvard Graduate School of Education.*

Index

Academic achievement: and adaptation, 94–95; of Asian immigrants, 42–43, 59; of boys, 92, 94–95, 105–106; effect of culture on, 57–58; effect of housework on, 37; effect of structure on, 57–58; effect of translating on, 36–37; and gender, 105–106; of girls, 92, 94–95, 105–106; of involuntary minorities, 43; of Latino immigrants, 95; overview of, 57; role of Chinese language schools in, 65; of voluntary minorities, 43. *See also* School

Adaptation: and academic achievement, 94–95; and attitude, 92, 96–97; and ethnic communities, 106; and ethnic identity, 102–103; and future aspirations, 95–96; and homework, 97; and parental control, 101–102; past research in, 93; and peer influences, 99–100; and perception of school safety, 100; and perception of support from school, 99; and racism, 101; research study of, 93–103; and retention of culture, 93, 106; and teachers' perceptions of student engagement, 98–99

African Americans: media use patterns of, 113; and racism toward Vietnamese immigrants, 47–48; teachers' perception of, 52–53

Age, distribution of housework and, 34

Americans: immigrant youth's segregation from, 20; Latino's perception of, 18; perceptions of Asian immigrants, 42

Anxiety: as effect of poverty, 20; of parents, 21; of Vietnamese immigrants, 51

Appiah, A., 2

Argueta-Bernal, G. A., 79

Asian immigrants: academic achievement of, 42–43, 59; Americans' perceptions of, 42; delinquency of, 50; leading theories of, 42–43; stereotype of, 42, 49, 50, 52–55, 63. *See also specific Asian groups*

Assimilation theories, 58

Attitude: of boys, 96–97; of Chinese immigrants, 97; of girls, 92, 96–97

Baldwin High School (California), 44–45

Bankson, C. L., 78

Behavior, and religion, 84–85

Boat people, 45

Boston, 75, 87

Boys: academic achievement of, 92, 94–95, 105–106; attitude of, 96–97; ethnic identity of, 102–103; future aspirations of, 95–96; versus girls in adaptation, 104; and homework, 97; housework of, 33–35; media use of, 123–124; opportunities for assimilation by, 106; parental control over, 101–102, 105; peer influences of, 99–100; and perception of school safety, 100; social capital of, 105; and teachers' perceptions of student engagement, 98–99

Brodie, M., 115

Brooklyn, 79

Brown, F., 92

Buddhism, 79

Care, for siblings, 29–30

Caribbean immigrants, 92

Catholicism, 79

CD player, number of youths with, 112

Celebrations, 67, 69

131

Kaiser Family Foundation, 115
Kluckhohn, C., 5

Language, segregation's effect on, 20
Latino immigrants: academic achievement of, 95; ethnic identity of,
102–103; ethnic language media
use of, 126–127; future aspirations
of, 95–96; importance of family to,
16; level of exposure to media of,
117; media content preferences of,
120–123; media ownership patterns
of, 115–116; media use patterns of,
113; parental control over, 102;
peer influences of, 100; perception
of Americans, 18; and perception
of school safety, 100; and religion,
79, 80–88; research study of housework and, 27–37; teachers' perception of, 52–53; types of housework
performed by, 29; vignettes about,
30–33
Lawrence, J., 26, 30
Li, X.-Y., 7, 11, 57
Literacy skills, effect of translating on,
36–37
Longitudinal Immigrant Student Adaptation study (LISA): overview, 7,
23; results of, 20, 93–103,
114–124
Lopez, N., 92
Louie, J., 7–8, 12–13, 111

Magazines, level of exposure to,
117–120
Maryland, 64
Math skills, effect of translating on,
36–37
Media: content preferences for,
120–123; and gender differences,
123–124; immigrant versus nonimmigrant ownership patterns of,
115; implications for use of,
128–129; influence of, 112; level of
exposure to, 111–112; ownership
trends of, 112, 115–116; parents'
involvement with use of, 129; ques-
tionable content of, 112; research
study of, 114–124; types of,

111–112; use patterns of, 113–114,
117. *See also specific media devices*
Mexican immigrants. *See* Latino immi-
grants
Model minority stereotype, 42, 49, 50,
52–55
Moral development, 35, 36, 67
Motivation, 52–53, 71
Multifinality, 76–77
Music: level of exposure to, 117–120;
sources of, 111

National Council of Associations of
Chinese Language Schools, 64
National Science Foundation, 7, 23
New York Chinese Schools, 64
Noam, G. G., 3

Ogbu, J. U., 59
Orellana, M. F., 6–7, 9–10, 25

Parental involvement: in Chinese language schools, 66, 69; in media
consumption, 129
Parenting skills, effect of American
culture on, 21
Parents: anxiety of, 21; control over
girls versus boys, 92, 101–102, 105;
depression of, 21; effects of Chinese language schools on, 67–71;
multiple obligations of, 21; support
for youth translators, 37; unavailability of, 21
Peace, 85
Peer influences, 99–100
Peer relationships: at Chinese language
schools, 70; importance of, 21–22;
of Vietnamese immigrants, 50–51
Pennsylvania, 64
Perez, C. C., 7, 10, 41
Pew Research Center, 77
Portes, A., 60, 92
Positive attitude, 92, 96–97
Poverty: coexistence of drugs and
school with, 20; effects of, 19–20;
as immigration stressor, 87–88;
number of youth living in, 19

Qin-Hilliard, D. B., 7, 12, 91

Racial integration, of Vietnamese immigrants, 51–52
Racism: and adaptation, 101; against Chinese immigrants, 63; girls' perception of, 93; as immigration stressor, 87–88; of teachers, 47–48; against Vietnamese immigrants, 47–48
Radio: level of exposure to, 117–120; number of youths with, 112, 115; ownership trends of, 115–117
Reading skills, effect of translating on, 36–37
Rebellion, 71
Recognition, 51
Relationships: function of, 22; with God, 86; importance of, 21–22
Relative functionalism, 42
Religion: an Latino immigrants, 80–88; and behavior, 84–85; benefits of, 76, 78–79; and Chinese immigrants, 79, 80–88; and culture, 84; and family, 84, 88; future research in, 88–89; and Haitian immigrants, 79, 80–88; importance of, 78, 80, 81–82; increase in prominence of, 77–78; and Latino immigrants, 79, 80–88; link to resilience, 76; percent of population that practices, 77; protective factors of, 78; research study of, 79–89; rituals of, 83–84, 88; and social support, 76; and Vietnamese immigrants, 78. See also Church; God
Resilience, 76
Rideout, V. J., 115
Risk and resilience framework, 77
Rituals, 83–84, 88
Roberts, D. F., 115
Role dissonance, 35
Rong, X. L., 92
Rumbaut, R. G., 92

San Francisco, 61
School: Chinese immigrants' dissatisfaction with, 65; Chinese immigrants' segregation in, 61; coexistence with poverty, 20; connection of Chinese language school to, 69; importance of, 21–22; importance of healthy environment in, 106–107; perception of safety in, 100; safety in, 100; segregation's effect on, 20; students' perception of support from, 99; Vietnamese immigrants' segregation in, 47. See also Academic achievement; Chinese language schools
Segregation: of Chinese immigrants, 61; effects of, 20; of Vietnamese immigrants, 47
Self-esteem, of Vietnamese immigrants, 51
Self-worth, 86
Sexual activity, 84–85
Sibling care, 29–30
Sleeping, 19
Social capital: of boys, 105; definition of, 60; effectiveness of, 72; of girls, 105
Social development, 35, 36
Social stratification. See Structure
Social support: effects of Chinese language schools on, 68–69; function of, 22; of girls, 104; and religion, 76
Southern California United Chinese School Association, 64
Spencer Foundation, 7, 23
Sports, 67
Stereotype, of Asian immigrants, 42, 49, 50, 52–55, 63
Stress, of immigration, 76–77, 87–88
Structure, 57–58
Student engagement, 98–99
Suárez-Orozco, C., 6, 7, 8, 9, 23, 35
Suárez-Orozco, M., 7, 23, 35
Sung, B. L., 70–71
Supplementary education. See Chinese language schools

Taiwanese immigrants, 64
Taoism, 79
Tape player, number of youths with, 112
Teachers: in Chinese language schools, 61, 63, 66; perceptions of African American youth, 52–53; perceptions of Latino youth, 52–53; perceptions of student engagement, 98–99; perceptions of Vietnamese

Back Issue/Subscription Order Form

Copy or detach and send to:

Jossey-Bass, A Wiley Company, 989 Market Street, San Francisco CA 94103-1741

Call or fax toll-free: Phone 888-378-2537; Fax 888-481-2665

Back Issues: Please send me the following issues at $29 each
(Important: please include issue ISBN)

_____

_____

$ _____   Total for single issues

$ _____   SHIPPING CHARGES: SURFACE   Domestic Canadian

	First Item	$5.00	$6.00
	Each Add'l Item	$3.00	$1.50

Please call for next day, second day, or international shipping rates.

Subscriptions   Please ❏ start ❏ renew my subscription to _New Directions for Youth Development_ at the following rate:

U.S.	❏ Individual $80	❏ Institutional $160
Canada	❏ Individual $80	❏ Institutional $200
All Others	❏ Individual $104	❏ Institutional $234
Online Subscription		❏ Institutional $176

**For more information about online subscriptions visit
www.interscience.wiley.com**

-- _____   Are you eligible for our **Student Subscription Rate**? Attach a copy of your current Student Identification Card and deduct 20% from the regular subscription rate.

$ _____   Total single issues and subscriptions (Add appropriate sales tax for your state for single issue orders. No sales tax for U.S. subscriptions. Canadian residents, add GST for subscriptions and single issues.)

❏ Payment enclosed (U.S. check or money order only)

❏ VISA ❏ MC ❏ AmEx # _____ Exp. Date _____

Your credit card payment will be charged to John Wiley & Sons.

Signature _____ Day Phone _____

❏ Bill Me (U.S. institutional orders only. Purchase order required.)

Purchase order # _____

Federal Tax ID13559302   **GST 89102 8052**

Name _____

Address _____

_____

Phone _____ E-mail _____

NEW DIRECTIONS FOR YOUTH DEVELOPMENT
IS NOW AVAILABLE ONLINE AT WILEY INTERSCIENCE

What is Wiley InterScience?

Wiley InterScience is the dynamic online content service from John Wiley & Sons delivering the full text of over 300 leading scientific, technical, medical, and professional journals, plus major reference works, the acclaimed *Current Protocols* laboratory manuals, and even the full text of select Wiley print books online.

What are some special features of Wiley InterScience?

Wiley InterScience Alerts is a service that delivers table of contents via e-mail for any journal available on Wiley InterScience as soon as a new issue is published online.
Early View is Wiley's exclusive service presenting individual articles online as soon as they are ready, even before the release of the compiled print issue. These articles are complete, peer-reviewed, and citable.
CrossRef is the innovative multi-publisher reference linking system enabling readers to move seamlessly from a reference in a journal article to the cited publication, typically located on a different server and published by a different publisher.

How can I access Wiley InterScience?

Visit http://www.interscience.wiley.com

Guest Users can browse Wiley InterScience for unrestricted access to journal Tables of Contents and Article Abstracts, or use the powerful search engine.
Registered Users are provided with a *Personal Home Page* to store and manage customized alerts, searches, and links to favorite journals and articles. Additionally, Registered Users can view free Online Sample Issues and preview selected material from major reference works.
Licensed Customers are entitled to access full-text journal articles in PDF, with select journals also offering full-text HTML.

How do I become an Authorized User?

Authorized Users are individuals authorized by a paying Customer to have access to the journals in Wiley InterScience. For example, a university that subscribes to Wiley journals is considered to be the Customer. Faculty, staff and students authorized by the university to have access to those journals in Wiley InterScience are Authorized Users. Users should contact their Library for information on which Wiley journals they have access to in Wiley InterScience.

ASK YOUR INSTITUTION ABOUT WILEY INTERSCIENCE TODAY!